TRUE HEART

INTUITIVE TAROT

TRUE HEART
INTUITIVE TAROT

RACHEL TRUE

HOUGHTON MIFFLIN HARCOURT

Boston · New York 2020

For information about permission to reproduce selections from this book,
write to trade.permissions@hmhco.com or to
Permissions, Houghton Mifflin Harcourt Publishing Company,
3 Park Avenue, 19th Floor, New York, New York 10016.

hmhbooks.com

Library of Congress Cataloging-in-Publication Data

Names: True, Rachel, author.
Title: True heart : intuitive tarot, guidebook and deck / Rachel True.
Description: Boston : Houghton Mifflin Harcourt, 2020. | Summary:
   "An exquisite tarot card deck and guidebook boxed set by Rachel True,
   best known as the co-star of the cult-classic movie The Craft"—Provided
   by publisher.
Identifiers: LCCN 2020004921 | ISBN 9781328566263 (pbk)
   Subjects: LCSH: Tarot.
Classification: LCC BF1879.T2 T78 2020 | DDC 133.3/2424—dc23
LC record available at https://lccn.loc.gov/2020004921

Book design by RAPHAEL GERONI
Illustrations by STEPHANIE SINGLETON

Printed in China
SCP 10 9 8 7 6 5 4 3 2 1

Dedicated to Pamela Coleman Smith
& all who came before.

We can predict the future when we know how the present moment evolved from the past.

—CARL JUNG

If you want to understand the secrets of the universe, think of it in terms of energy, frequency, and vibration.

—NIKOLA TESLA

CONTENTS

INTRODUCTION

True Heart Intuitive Tarot is a practical guide to connect you to your intuition through the use of a deck of tarot cards. Whether you are a longtime reader who is always keeping up with the latest word in tarot or a newbie just getting your feet wet, this book is for you.

When people find out I read tarot, the first question I inevitably get asked, perhaps justifiably, is, "You got into tarot because you played a witch in *The Craft*, right?"

Nope! While it's true actress Fairuza Balk and I were *The Craft* castmates who had a prior interest in the esoteric (for a while she owned Pan Pipes, a Wiccan store in Hollywood), I myself have never identified as a pagan or a witch. Although, to the more conservative-minded, I may have habits and rituals that appear . . . earthy. A tad witchy. I'm not a total muggle; I just really hate labels.

My tarot decks are among my closest and best forever friends. I'm a lifelong practitioner, and part of a movement committed to demystifying and destigmatizing esoteric studies. The tarot tells the story of humanity, giving you insight into yourself by helping you clarify the now and make better choices for the future. They're like a shrink in a box and spiritual Xanax all rolled into one.

Can tarot cards tell your future? The cards themselves are simply wood pulp and ink; the "magic" is in their ability to tap into your unconscious desires and fears. Tarot is exceptional at laying out *possible* future outcomes based on present energies. However, nothing is set in stone; your future is always shifting based on your choices. We are always becoming.

What you get with tarot is straightforward, practical advice to help you move forward by uncovering the unconscious patterns that are holding you back. A good reading will give you incisive information as to which areas of your life are working and which need course correction. Active participation in implementing change is entirely up to the person being read.

Carl Jung, one of the fathers of modern psychology, was fascinated with tarot and utilized the cards in his practice. He described them as a tool for integration of self through connection to the collective unconsciousness (defined as "unconscious psyche, common to all mankind"—Jung).

Seeing into the unknown (in this case, the inner you) and knowing how to actively shift energy to work for you is an awesome skill. We all have access to innate clairvoyance and intuition, but most of us tuned it out in early childhood. With the help of the tarot, you can dial back into your own frequency and fine-tune it.

As a precocious five-year-old, I picked up Jung's *Man and His Symbols* from my dad's imposing bookcase, and my curiosity turned into a fixation. None of it was startlingly clear to me as a grade-schooler, but that book made me aware that most fairy tales have deeper, hidden meanings; a story can be a tool to help us process life. What would my story look like?

I was given my first tarot deck by a family friend, and recognized the symbols on the cards from Jung's book. My father, forever shrouded behind a wall of tarry smoke, saw me poring over my cards and told me stories of his Hungarian Jewish gypsy grandmother. "Maybe you inherited her gifts. They say she could tell the future and when people were going to die."

I don't know when anyone's going to die, but even at a young age, I did seem to have a knack for picking up on people's thoughts, something I found scary and others found annoying. People tend to dwell on the negative, and they don't realize that this manifests as a swirly cloud of muddled energy around them. It took me a little while to keep unrequested advice to myself.

When I started reading tarot for people other than my friends, one of the first things I realized was how rampant the disease of anxiety was among most Americans.

I want you to be gentle with yourself when approaching tarot, and the ensuing self-integration. Negative thoughts (often represented by the reversed Ace of Swords or the 9 of Swords in tarot) indicate a stressed-out mind. If you're in a tight spot and things look bleak in your world right now, start to become aware—without judgment—of how your inner voice sounds. How do you speak to yourself? By picking up this book, you've already made a decision to shift the dynamic.

Tarot is a personal journey; there is no right and no wrong way to do this once you have the concepts and card interpretations personalized.

While there are common keywords and interpretations, my personal understanding of the dynamic layers of each card continues to evolve and expand. I hope the same will be true for you.

When *The Craft* came out, a few now well-known African American actresses made a point of telling me they flat-out passed on the script because of the subject matter, to which I thought, *Good, it wasn't your part anyway.* Growing up in the '70s, the word *occult*, from the Latin *occultus*, meaning something hidden or difficult to see, was synonymous with satanic rituals and vomiting split pea soup. Manon, the spirit the girls in *The Craft* worshipped, is not based on any known deity; it is the name of a spring in France; the producers were wary of unknowingly calling something up. Unfortunately, a lot of people are still scared off from exploring tarot or anything earthy, and it doesn't help that shoddy psychics and spiritual fraudsters use tarot to prey on those in crisis. Most people were as skeptical of Miss Cleo's claim of a "free tarot reading" as they were of tarot itself, and for good reason. Tarot isn't about lifting curses and luring lovers back your way. If a tarot reader needs a fresh egg, some of your hair, and/or $10,000 to clear your energy, you've entered the bullshit zone.

One of the most practical reasons for reading tarot is the balance it helps you attain by outwardly displaying your behavioral patterns while attuning you to the frequency and choices your spirit and soul are guiding you toward. Tarot cards alert you when things are veering off-path and help silence the looping tape of negative self-talk by offering you an alternative way of thinking. The cards will cheer you on, celebrate your victories, and show you the ray of hope already living inside you just when you need it.

Developing and trusting your intuition is the most important skill the tarot teaches, and it's the key to reading the cards accurately. They're designed to help you free yourself; the more you fly, the higher you vibrate, and the clearer the story the cards tell. That's the beauty of tarot; you don't need any special talents. Just your open mind. You can pick up your own deck, clear your energy, and feel empowered doing it. The only thing you'll be summoning up is your own intuition, insight, and connection to spirit.

A common theme in the tarot is the duality of mankind: our intellectual side and our animal side. When we face both the intellectual high vibe and the baser, animalistic low vibe, we allow our true self to lead. From there, the soul's purpose is revealed. Once this happens, it becomes harder and harder to continue with low-vibe behavior that's dragging life down. I refer to tarot as a shrink in a box for a reason. When it's late at night and spinning anxiety is keeping you up or a decision is confusing you, tarot can give you the clarity you seek.

I would like to thank some of the tarot practitioners, mentors (by way of their books), and other magic workers who shaped my practice and still sculpt my tarot journey and advance my evolution as a reader. These include Mary K. Greer, whose many workbooks I treasure; Starhawk for *The Spiral Dance*; Rachel Pollack for her wisdom; Karen Vogel, Jonathan Tenney, and Vicki Noble for creating the Motherpeace deck and spread; and most of all, thank you to Pamela Colman Smith for creating the art and long-enduring archetypes of the classic Rider-Waite-Smith deck.

GETTING STARTED

Tapping Into Your Intuition

One of the most important parts of preparing to read tarot is getting centered and shutting out the noise of the day. Find a comfortable, distraction-free environment to practice your tarot. Try the steps below before you jump full steam into readings.

Step 1: Get Focused

Take a few moments to shake off the day's tribulations. Light a candle or some incense, if possible, to aid in focus and help carry intentions out into the world. Choose a candle color that is soothing to you (and remove the price sticker, if it has one).

Shut off your phone, laptop, and television. Feel free to put on relaxing meditative background music, if you like. Distraction, whether intentional or not, is the number one intuition blocker. This is the beginning of releasing behaviors that no longer serve you.

Step 2: Get Comfortable

Relax. This may be a new concept to wrap your head around, but it's one of the most integral steps toward calming anxiety, finding peace, and forging a connection to your higher self. If you were once an over-scheduled child and now find yourself an overscheduled adult, learn to dedicate time, no matter how little an amount, to your personal well-being.

In tarot, the element of water symbolizes our inner emotional life. One of the simplest ways to relax and release tensions you may have subconsciously stored during the day is to soak in a tub or take a shower. You can add inexpensive Epsom salts, which help pull toxins from the body. You can also add essential oils for their various relaxing or invigorating energies.

Step 3: Get Centered

Breathe. Breath is life. One of the quickest ways to clear out mind chatter and let your higher self get a word in edgewise is to practice mindfulness through simple breathing techniques. They're an incredibly helpful tool in relaxing the central nervous system, which in turn can slow anxious thoughts. Tight, binding clothing, suffocating bras, and even some jewelry can affect breath, which will in turn affect your ability to relax and connect with your inner self.

GET CENTERED BREATHING EXERCISE/MEDITATION

This exercise works wonders in all sorts of stress-inducing circumstances, and you can do it almost anywhere without calling attention to yourself. Try it at home first.

Begin by sitting on the floor, cross-legged or in any position comfortable to you. Use pillows or other support items if needed. Close your eyes and take a 7-second-long breath in through your nose, then release it in a 7-second-long exhalation through your mouth; repeat this several times. While you're doing this, imagine a shimmer of white light expanding from the top of your head, your crown chakra, all the way around your whole body. Imagine this light infusing you with warmth and filling your entire body, inside and out. Be mindful of your breath, and continue to extend each inhalation and exhalation. Note any thoughts that come into your mind, and send them away without judgment. If anxiety begins to creep in, refocus by returning to the physical feeling and sensation of the air flowing in and out of your nose and mouth. Repeat for as little or long as you feel you need to, or as time permits.

LEARNING TO PICK UP ENERGY

Expand on the previous breathing exercise by adding, one at a time, the people, places, and things in your life. Let's see how they make you vibrate.

Begin by sitting in a comfortable position and do the breathing exercise as before. But this time, when you're feeling centered and relaxed, imagine a small square on the wall, and inside it, a projected movie showing the main relationship in your life, whomever that might be with. This can be a romantic partner, or maybe it's your mother, or a close friend. Think about your memories of that person, and visualize them as though you are watching your memories in a film. As you watch, note what sensation you feel in your body. Is it high and tingly, or low and tuggy, or somewhere in between?

If the energy in you and the room is zingy and vibrating on a fun frequency or heart wavelength, that's a sign that the connection's in a good place. If you notice a downshift or feel drained, that is your intuition letting you know the dynamic in that relationship needs attention. When you follow the cues your intuition gives you, your higher self's voice will rise and resonate inside you and through the cards.

Continue to do this exercise with other major relationships in your life. When you're finished, note where your energy is vibrating. If you have low-vibe connections, don't let it bring you down. You can pull some tarot cards for advice on how to move into a higher vibe, or let go gracefully.

Know that you don't have to make any choices or changes yet, unless you're inspired to. This exercise is simply to identify and acknowledge low- and high-vibe relationship dynamics using your intuition. The more you dialogue with your higher self, the less you'll naturally be inclined to partake in low-vibe indulgences.

GET GROUNDED IN NATURE

Another way to get centered is to stand barefoot on grass or earth to ground your energy. According to a study published in the *Journal of Environmental and Public Health* in January 2012, researchers found that when test subjects did this, there was a "rapid activation of the parasympathetic nervous system and corresponding deactivation of the sympathetic nervous system." The study found that this reduced stress and body inflammation, which means a more intuitive you. Earth, represented by the suit of Discs, is where tangible manifestation takes place; it makes sense that having some contact with the earth would provide benefit.

The same principle applies to a small amount of sun a day. We need the sun's rays to synthesize vitamin D, and without enough of this vitamin, the body suffers symptoms that mimic depression and other illnesses. Even if you live in a concrete jungle, there's a park bench somewhere with your name on it. Just five minutes of sunshine a day can help shift your mood.

The Back Story

Very little is truly known about the exact origins of the tarot, despite its enduring popularity. Some trace the cards back to ancient Egypt, while historical records show Italian nobles began using them in the early fifteenth century. They were used as playing cards, as fortune-telling cards, and as a storytelling device among courtiers who could not otherwise voice their romantic or lusty desires.

The first officially noted European tarot deck was called the Visconti-Sforza, named after Duke Francesco Sforza, Duke of Milan, and his second wife, Bianca Maria Visconti. Since then, tarot has evolved, undergoing many transformations including the number of cards in a deck and their meanings. Early and modern cards retain heavy Judeo-Christian undertones, which are parables for our current joys, dilemmas, and struggles of faith.

Modern tarot evolved rapidly in large part due to the spiritualist movement that began in the late twentieth century. The Rider-Waite-Smith deck is the standard for its Jungian archetypes and accessible themes. It was created by Arthur Edward Waite, a member of the Hermetic Order of the Golden Dawn, a secret esoteric society, and published by Rider in London in 1909. Pamela Colman Smith, the artist and a Golden Dawn member herself, went uncredited until very recently.

Colman Smith's contributions to the esoteric arts are beautifully told in a new book, *Pamela Colman Smith: The Untold Story*. One of my early tarot inspirations, Mary K. Greer, had a hand in the book. Before widespread internet availability, Mary's workbooks immeasurably helped sculpt my and many a tarot reader's practice and outlook. Her devotion to helping Pamela Colman Smith reclaim her long overdue place in the legacy of tarot is much appreciated.

I found myself relating and even calling on conversation with Ms. Colman Smith many times during the writing of this book and creation of my deck. Like myself, she was a mixed woman living a rather bohemian life among artists and provocateurs, working in the theatrical arts and other visual media at the height of the spiritual revolution of the day. Heady stuff for women of color, who, post-slavery, were designated to domestic labor or sewing work, if they were lucky and skilled. My deck is highly influenced by the enduring Rider-Waite-Smith tarot imagery created over a century ago, because the imagery tells the story succinctly, and the art is rife with touchstones of everyday human existence. Colman Smith was able to transcend what the times prescribed for her gender, skin color, and station, making her a true renaissance woman.

Choosing a Tarot Deck

Despite the persistent myth that you must be gifted your first or any subsequent tarot deck, feel free to pick one out right now, unless you *want* to wait to be gifted one. Tarot by nature is active, not passive—it's a giving and receiving of energy. Why be passive in obtaining a deck, or anything else you truly desire?

Picking a specific deck is a little like asking how you prefer your tea: bitter and black with a squeeze of lemon? Or light and thick with cream and sugar? It boils down to personal taste, and the multitude of decks available means there's something for everyone and every mood.

Tarot works symbiotically with religion, analytical therapy, and your own inner knowing. Most people who read tarot regularly tend to have a collection of decks for display or for when their main reading deck gets cranky. Sometimes the theme of a certain deck will fit an occasion or query, and an ancillary deck can be a better fit. Sometimes you're just more receptive to receiving information in the way a certain deck delivers it, so it's good to have options.

Once you learn the traditional themes of the cards, you'll have a foundation to build on, even if your deck was designed by Lisa Frank and bears no resemblance to traditional decks. Some decks utilize imagery that initially may be confusing if you don't know the language of tarot. For example, the lovely and thoroughly modern Delta Enduring Tarot, which comes out of New Orleans and Southern tradition, replaces Cups (water) with Oysters; Discs (earth) with Oak Trees; Swords (air) with Moths; and Wands (fire) with Cast-Iron Skillets. The elemental energy matches up with the traditional Rider-Waite-Smith tarot, even if the imagery is completely different. It's important to find imagery that speaks to you; it doesn't matter if someone else doesn't like your deck's artwork if it resonates for you.

You do not have to sleep with your deck under your pillow, but you can if you want (it's not very comfortable). You are free to make up your own rules and interact with your deck any way you see fit. Much of magic is what you *believe* and the energy you put toward and behind your intention. It's up to you to spread your higher self's spiritual wings and explore any number of ways that help you connect to your intuition.

Care and Feeding of Your Deck

Decks I use regularly are stored in ornate carved wooden boxes, which display them and protect their energy. You should do what feels comfortable and natural for you, so long as your cards are in a place where others won't disturb them and they won't get dusty. I like to wrap mine in antique natural-fiber cloths, such as cotton or silk, and then I perform readings on top of the same cloth. You can do the same, or leave them in their original box.

You can sage your deck to clear its energy before readings. I like to place my crystals on my decks or wave bundled or loose black sage, mugwort, or palo santo to clear out low-vibe energy. White sage is becoming endangered and is not the most environmentally sound choice. Some people sage periodically, while others sage every time they use their decks or feel a low-vibe energy.

If the cards are coated, they can be wiped down every so often with a soft cloth and plain water. Once in a while, I'll use a mixture of plain water and Florida Water, an energy-clearing solution you can find at esoteric shops. When a deck seems to stop working altogether, that's the perfect time to cleanse yourself and the deck.

Occasionally a deck will become impossible to read with, no matter how well you've cared for it. This is a sign that A) you may be doing too many consecutive readings and need a break to process; B) your deck needs a vacation for a few weeks to recharge; or C) the deck is done. When this is the case, you can keep the deck for posterity, in remembrance of how it served you and to honor the knowledge you've gained. Usually when a deck's gone off, my personal ritual is to bind the deck with twine and submerge the cards in a bowl of water for a few days. I then mush the paper into pulp, form the pulp into a ball, and bury it in my yard. That's just me, though, and may or may not work for your needs. Remember, you make your own rules.

Setting Up an Altar

Dedicating a piece of your personal space as an altar creates a place for you to focus and set your daily intentions. On a subconscious level, when you walk by your altar, it will remind you to pay attention to messages from your higher self and spirit. It's a space to honor your ancestors and the contributions they made to your existence.

The altar can be as big or small as you like. Try placing a cloth and a special candle on the intended area to help delineate the space for you. A living plant or fresh flowers placed on the altar are nice touches and symbolize fertile new growth.

Add special items that hold personal value, and images of things you aspire to. This is a living vision board, in a sense, so when you light your altar candle, picture the flame carrying your wishes up and out into the universe.

You can store your deck, sage, and the candle you use for tarot readings on the altar as well. If you're doing a one-card tarot pull for daily guidance, pull the card and place it at the center of your altar. If you're doing a reading for yourself and having trouble with specific cards, place them on your altar until they reveal themselves to you.

Keep a Physical Notebook

One of the best ways to track your progress, from learning interpretations to clocking cycles of repeating cards and how they play out in your life, is to keep a dedicated notebook or tarot journal. Patterns and progress are much easier to identify when there's a record. I realize it's tempting to go digital all the way, but think of this as your own personal grimoire and tarot diary. This is where you can record not just a picture of the card, but your feelings around the reading. You can hand-draw symbols with the card names, or get creative and collage pictures of your readings.

You can use one book as a learning workbook, just for your initial impression of the cards' interpretations, and a separate journal to record your readings and spreads, or do a combination journal.

Connecting to Your Tarot Cards Using the Actor's Way

One of the best ways to break the code and understand the language of tarot is to develop a personal relationship with each and every one of those seventy-eight cards. While that may sound overwhelming, it can be accomplished in a few hours, utilizing actor's methods for understanding a character and memorizing lines with little to no advance notice.

You certainly don't need to become a thespian to practice tarot, but you can borrow a page from their book to intimately get to know and lock in the meanings of the cards.

Actors use imagination to entice their brains and central nervous systems into believing they're actually in situations that they're not. It's called sense memory, and when utilized correctly, it lets an actor relate the feelings they need to evoke on camera back to experiences in their own lives that produced a similar feeling. This creates an adrenaline or dopamine surge, enabling performers to believe and act like they're freezing and climbing Mount Everest, when in reality, they're on a backlot in Burbank and it's eighty degrees.

Tarot helps us identify and release triggering emotions. The word *emotion* comes from the Latin root *emovere*, meaning "to move out, remove, agitate." Emotions are feelings in a living, active state. The key is not only thinking intellectually about a card, but experiencing the *emotion* the card evokes and identifying the specific feeling that emotion invokes. That "feeling" gives the essence of the card, locks in the meaning, and taps you into the card's energy. And just like no two actors will play the same role the same way, no two tarot readers bring the same life experience to their interpretation of a card.

The Actor's Way Exercise

Before you look up the interpretations or begin throwing cards, this exercise is an ideal way to fast-track your connection to your deck. For seasoned practitioners, it can still provide a benefit, illuminating how far your understanding of the card's energy has evolved over the years.

Take your deck and pull a card. Start with the top card from your new unshuffled deck, if you like order and methodology, or shuffle and pull from anywhere if you're feeling lucky. Place the card faceup in front of you. Really look at the card. Note your reactions to the following questions in your journal:

- Imagine you are the character on the card. Play it out like a film in your head. How do you feel?

- What emotion does the card imagery evoke for you on a visceral, gut level?
- Now, with a more analytical mind, glance again at the card. What do you see, specifically? What are the details? How do you feel about your own energetic shift up or down, in reaction to the card?
- Does this card make you happy? Or does it remind you of a side of yourself you don't particularly like?

If you have a negative reaction, explore what the upside of the card's energy might be. Even the dreaded 3 of Swords can be a celebration of release from past heartache. Notice how your personal energy shifts, from low vibe to neutral to high, just by imagining yourself experiencing release or success.

Let's use The Fool, the first card of the deck, as an example. Even if you're the most responsible type A person in the world, you can probably think of at least one time when you went after what you wanted without fully thinking through the consequences and, despite the risks, ended up scoring big. The exhilarating feeling you have associated with that moment is the high vibe Fool.

Write down as little or as much as you're inspired to. It can be a few words or as many paragraphs as you want about what the imagery evokes and the feelings brought up by the card you pulled.

When you're finished writing, look up the card interpretation to see how your feelings about what the card might represent match up. Note similarities and differences in your notebook. Write down the keywords or a few phrases that resonate from the interpretations. Continue to do this for as many cards as you like, or until you've eventually made it through the entire deck.

You can do this over an extended period of time or in a few days. The sooner you make it through all seventy-eight cards, the quicker your intuition can understand how combinations of cards work together to tell a story in advanced spreads.

Your particular feelings around the card you pull will give you an insight into yourself as well as imbed the "feeling" of the tarot interpretation and build a connection between you and your intuition. Going off dry keywords doesn't allow for the exchange of energy between you and the cards. This energy is the very thing that opens up your intuition.

You'll come to find that the exact same card can have a completely different slant for two different people, or even the same person at different stages of their individual journey.

Continue to remain open to deeper levels of dialogue and more nuanced understanding of your cards. New and expanded meanings will come through the more you use your deck and your intuition awakens.

DIGGING INTO YOUR DECK

There are seventy-eight cards in a deck: twenty-two Major Arcana and fifty-six Minor Arcana. This number can seem daunting until you break down the groupings.

The Major Arcana are numbered 0 to 21. They begin with The Fool, number 0, and tell the story of the archetypal hero's journey, peeling back the layers of the human condition from birth to rebirth. The story of The Fool's quest to follow bliss to great heights or tremendous folly is retold in countless movies, songs, and stories. Our collective desires, triumphs, heartbreaks, disillusionment, despair, rebirth, resolution, and completion are all represented. The Major Arcana end with The World (which is numbered 21 but is technically the twenty-second card, since there is a 0 card). Think of these cards as indicators that major cycles are moving in or out.

Quite often, these concepts can seem like abstract, intangible ideas. That's where the Minor Arcana come in, to help fill in the blanks and let you know how these grand conceptual cards play out.

Minor Arcana cards represent the day-to-day ups and down we encounter on our paths. These cards succinctly reveal telling information about life's practicalities and mundanities. The Minor Arcana are divided into four suits, each of which represents an element. Each suit has fourteen cards, numbered Ace through 10, as well as four corresponding court/face cards, almost like a regular deck of playing cards.

Overall, when you receive a Major Arcana in a spread, it carries more weight than the Minor Arcana cards you've drawn, and asks you pay extra attention to its message. Note the Minor Arcana cards surrounding the Major Arcana cards in readings, as they're clues to where this Major energy is affecting your day-to-day life.

Tarot by the Numbers

Being familiar with the energy of a tarot card's number makes it easier to quickly intuit meanings in the card, as well as the whole spread. If you pull more than one of the same number in a spread, pay close attention. Each number carries a frequency.

ACE or 0: potential, possibilities, beginnings, new cycles, ego

2: balance, tranquility, an inner experience moving toward reunion of self/ reconciliation with another, diplomacy, harmony, partnership, duality

3: growth, movement, groups, creation, triangles, abundance, change, creative expression, integration, expansion, jealousy

4: stability, foundations, protection, practicality, boundaries, security, safety, control, rigidity

5: change, conflict, expansion, instability, movement, courage, growth through adversity, challenges

6: active balance, harmony, beauty, resolution after the conflict of the 5s, compassion, peaks, peace, recovery from adversity

7: reflection, choices, introspection, delusion, inspection, spirituality, reassessment, illusions, patience, potential

8: movement, rededication, hard work, psychic dreams, energy, karmic pulls, agreeable changes, strength, reward

9: plateaus, fruition, a final push, nearing the end of the journey, endings, dark night of the soul

10: culmination, ending, completion, rebirth, beginnings, group energy, new cycles

The Four Suits

Like a regular deck of playing cards has Hearts, Diamonds, Clubs, and Spades, the tarot has Cups, Wands, Swords, and Discs (though some decks use different symbols). The four suits, or elements, are where our hopes, dreams, and desires are played out and manifested. The Major Arcana are laced with visual and allegorical references to the elements explored in the Minor Arcana.

Cups (Water, Emotions, Feelings)

Pleasure, feelings, love, dreams, happiness, psychic opening, intuition, receptivity

Cups represent our emotional inner life, feelings, and the ability to express them.

As a personality archetype, these are the lovers and peacekeepers . . . who can drown in their own emotions.

Astrological signs: Scorpio, Cancer, Pisces

Wands (Fire, Energy, Desires)

Passion, energy, fiery life-force energy, intuition, invention, creativity, growth, action, forward motion

Wands represent our fiery life-force energy and the actions that help manifest ideas into tangible reality.

As a personality archetype, these are the artists and forward-thinkers, creatives who can overwhelm others in an effort to get their way.

Astrological signs: Leo, Aries, Sagittarius

Swords (Air, Mind, Intellect)

Intellect, mind, analytical thoughts, mental clarity, cutting away what no longer serves

Swords represent our intellectual life and the ability to make clear, conscious decisions.

As a personality archetype, these are the brilliant thinkers, eternally curious and occasionally emotionally disconnected.

Astrological signs: Libra, Gemini, Aquarius

Discs (Earth, Outer Life, Possessions)

Instinct, finances, money, tangible things, abundance, security, work, career

Discs are the only suit that represents the external physical world and the tangible attainable things in it.

As a personality archetype, this is the practical, pragmatic thinker who grows and occasionally hoards their possessions.

Astrological signs: Taurus, Virgo, Capricorn

Putting the Suit Energy and Numerical Value Together

Each card in both the Major and Minor Arcanas has a numerical value, and this number's vibration is affected by its corresponding suit's energy.

For example, let's say you pull the 2 of Discs. We know the number 2 represents decisions and balance. We know that the suit of Discs concerns money and physical things. Without even looking at the card's interpretation or seeing any imagery, you already now have a basic understanding of what you're dealing with, likely that practical concerns, like finding a balance between work and social life, or balance in financial considerations, are at hand.

Let's break down another card using this method, say the 4 of Cups. Cups are emotions, and the number 4 represents stability, building a strong foundation, and safety. Depending where the reader is at mentally, this could be a comforting card, as in you're feeling secure and grounded emotionally. Alternatively, if you're feeling off balance, this card may make you feel like protecting yourself and hiding out. Bear in mind that no card is an island; unless you're strictly doing one-card pulls, each card is only part of the story being told.

The Court Cards

Also called People, or Face cards, these are often the most challenging cards for new tarot students to grasp. Court cards may represent actual people around you or different facets of your own personality, or can embody the general energy currently around you.

In traditional decks, the Court is stacked with male energy: Pages (or Jacks), Knights, Queens, and Kings. In the True Heart Tarot deck,

I've balanced the genders by swapping Pages for Princesses and Knights for Princes. This makes them a little less warfaring, and members of the same family, with all the hierarchy issues and baggage any family contains. It's helpful to ignore each card's gender and hair color, and pay more attention to the suit, hierarchy, and energetic value.

No matter the suit:

The Princess carries the potential for their particular suit's element, or energy. Being the youngest family member, they tend to have an inquisitive energy and come bearing messages or asking questions. They can offer a fresh approach on situations stumping more jaded eyes. Apprentices to almost all they encounter, Princesses can often signify a student, or anyone engaging in a new course of study. In low vibe, this archetype can be immature in how they approach the world.

The Prince represents energy in action and has a tendency to exert their will in a more aggressive way, without thought to the repercussions. This can often work to their advantage, as fortune favors the brave. Princes can represent any gender ideology. It's the person in your life who rushes in without fully thinking things through, who is maybe a little too assertive in stating their needs. In low vibe, the Prince can rep a person full of passivity who's draining their potential.

The Queen represents our inner intuitive knowing and acquired wisdom. Their actions and attitudes tend to play out in less overt ways than the tarot King's actions and attitudes do. While this may be a gender stereotype, make no mistake, the King would be nowhere without the Queen's steady hand to help guide him. As a leader, the Queen knows when to draw a line in the sand, put her foot down, and put someone in their place, but she tends to work in subtle ways and with grace. In low vibe, a Queen can be overly critical, demanding, and petty.

The King represents his specific suit's energies mastered, clarified, and actively applied. The King is comfortable at the top; he's earned that position with the help of his Queen counterpart. Though he may lean into a more willful energy, utilizing an aggressive stance when needed, his decisions will benefit all parties involved. As with the other cards, a

King may represent a man or a woman around you, or the more active and more passive sides of yourself. In low vibe, a King can be patronizing, myopic, and judgmental.

If you receive a number of Court cards in a reading, there may be a lot of people up in your business. You may be utilizing all facets of your personality, but you could also feel emotionally out of balance. An abundance of Court cards may be telling you it's time to stop listening to so many other people's opinions, as it's causing confusion, or that it's time to focus on integrating the various yous roaming around your head.

Reading "Reversals," or the "Low Vibe" of Cards

For some readers, when a card is pulled from the deck upside down, it's a reversal, or sometimes it's called "poorly aspected." Generally, a reversed card can be interpreted as the opposite energy of what the card normally means, when drawn right-side up.

Some readers will leave these cards upside down, while others, including myself, turn all the cards right-side up and depend on intuition, and the card's position in a spread, to determine its vibration. There are positive and negative energies in all the cards. Each has what I call a lower vibration and a higher vibration; a light and a dark side; a yin and a yang. When you pull a card, be truthful with yourself, without judgment: Is this card speaking to your high vibe or your low vibe?

We often make choices we know aren't in our best interest, then feel guilty about them and spin in anxiety. That self-induced stress actively blocks intuition. Tarot reveals truths, so if you're involved in situations you intuitively know aren't ideal for your mental health or physical well-being, you won't be able to hide your true feelings from the tarot.

Shuffling

If you are not a great shuffler, you will be after spending some time with your cards. If your lack of shuffling abilities is causing you anxiety, don't worry, there are other methods (though I'm sure there's a YouTube video for that).

The important thing about shuffling is that it's a time of focus. Think about the question you are asking the card. If you are putting cards into a spread, think of the position the card falls into. Continue shuffling until you feel connected to your deck and your purpose. Then, traditionally, you set your deck down and cut it into three piles (some use two piles, or just one—it's personal choice). Stack the piles back up in any order you like. Pull cards off the top of the deck.

Rather than shuffle, some readers swirl their cards around in front of them while thinking of their question. You can then pull randomly from the swirled cards, or arrange them back into one stack and pull from the top of the stack.

There are many other ways to pick cards, so go with whichever methodology feels organic to you. Sometimes, you won't know which pile is supposed to go on top or which card to pick. Let the stress go, pick a pile, and trust that the right information, at the right time, will come up for you.

One helpful way to choose is to run your hand over the piles or swirled cards. See which cards give off some heat. I've received what feels like electrical zaps or energy coming off certain piles or cards—those are the ones I go for.

While shuffling, when a card jumps out of the deck, note it to inform the reading, or use this card as a one-card reading. You can also place this jumper card in the number 1 position of a spread and keep shuffling. This card fell out for a reason, so treat it as special. Some readers will do an entire tarot spread without purposefully ever drawing a card; they just wait for cards to fall out of the deck. That seems like a prolonged process to me, but do what feels natural to you, and develop your own method.

When laying down cards pulled from the deck for a spread, some readers lay them facedown and reveal them one by one; others place them faceup from the start.

There is no right or wrong; it's all personal choice. The only rules are the ones you set for yourself.

Pulling Clarifying Cards

Some readers choose to immediately pull clarifying cards, which are extra cards pulled from the deck to help supplement the reading. When first learning tarot, a lot of extra cards can be confusing and diffuse the message your higher self is trying to deliver. Once you're more familiar with your deck, clarifying cards can certainly be helpful, but for now I encourage you to sit with the cards you've drawn and tune into the story being told. If you get nothing, make sure you've looked up all the interpretations for the cards in question to gain new insights before pulling extra cards.

Unexpected revelations may strike you when you put in the work. Throwing spread after spread until the desired cards pop up is not tarot—it's playing Go Fish. Sometimes when we don't "get" it, that's a sign there's blocked energy or an unwillingness to examine a side of ourselves.

Reading for Other People

Reading for your friends as well as yourself can be a very helpful way to learn tarot, so here's a few tips. Tarot reading can be invasive by nature; you're peeking into your own or someone else's energy. Reading and reflecting this energy back to someone can be intimate and jarring to both parties. Remember to be judicious with your words, and clear in how you deliver information. Don't rely too heavily on what you already know about your pal. Let the cards and your intuition guide you. Your personal take on what others should or should not be doing with their life is not part of the equation, unless they're specifically asking for your personal opinion. Occasionally, there may be certain topics you'll want to avoid or tread lightly around if they're especially triggering. It's also important to remember that a tarot reading will not fix all of your friend's problems, or even your own.

It's okay to look up card definitions when reading for yourself or friends. In fact, you should do that when first beginning your practice. However, if you're planning to charge money for readings, you should know the cards inside and out, period. Charging money says to the world you understand the system of tarot thoroughly and are confident in your ability to interpret a spread's message. If you have to reach for this book or any other in the middle of a reading, you can't back up that claim. Look up all the definitions you want to compare and contrast once you're off the clock.

TAROT SPREADS

Spreads are the Rosetta Stone for tarot. A spread is interpreted by a combination of the card's (or cards') placement, its meaning, and your own intuition. The cards work in synergy with one another, and their interpretation is shaded by the surrounding cards. If tarot cards are the vehicle, the spread is the road map.

There are as many layouts as you can imagine, and you can even create your own. I'll go over a few simple spreads, and a few of my favorites.

Feel free to try any of these spreads with just the Major Arcana to get a power message highlighting the big energy in play; otherwise, use the entire deck for a fuller picture. If interpreting a spread proves troublesome, place it on your altar or designated tarot space to ruminate and create a living connection between you and the cards' message. When you walk by it throughout the day, be open to receiving new insight.

Before "throwing a spread" for yourself or someone else, focus on a question or situation at hand. You can be general, but with tarot, the more specific the question, the better, and be mindful of your phrasing. This can inform and give a reference for the cards that come up. There are no hard-and-fast rules, so do what your intuition guides you to do.

The important thing to remember with tarot is that nothing is set in stone. If you see something you don't like in the cards, look at it as an opportunity to shift behaviors and change course. A change in mind-set and attitude can shift the outcome.

There are a lot of cards, and it's easy to get confused with a big spread if you don't know what to pay attention to. Patterns can give you layers that help you intuit your spread's deeper meaning. The first thing to do is get an overview of what elemental suit, if any, dominates the reading. For example, if your spread has mostly Cup cards, emotional entanglements may be at the forefront of your mind. If your question is business related and you pull a lot of Cups, it's a clue that your emotions are factoring into work situations.

Patterns inside the spread help inform the spread as a whole. No cards are autonomous, unless you're doing a one-card reading. For example, if you do a three-card love spread, and get The Lovers in card position 1, and cards 2 and 3 are heavy cards, you must take into account the position of The Lovers compared to the message of the cards around it (in this case, the cards could be telling you there are difficulties around your love connection). Alternatively, if you pull The

Lovers and it's surrounded in a spread by happy, upbeat cards from any suit, this could indicate a romantic liaison with promise.

One-Card Daily Pull Guidance Spread

This is a short and sweet way to start off the day. Shuffle your deck, facedown, and think about your goals for the day. Pull one card off the top or from anywhere in the deck and place it faceup or facedown in front of you. Whichever card you pull is a guideline: note its message, and remember to remain open to how its influence affects you throughout the day.

What If You Have a Low-Vibe or Bummer Reaction to Your Daily Pull?

We give so much thought to the negative during the day, it spirals us down. Why not let tarot guide you to a high-vibe spiral up? One of the ways to get in touch with intuition is to begin to recognize feelings and release them, rather than suppressing them and letting them fester. Releasing, rather than reliving, disinvites the feeling from settling in and undermining progress.

One-Card, One-Question Spread

This is basically the same as the One-Card Daily Guidance Spread, but rather than looking for blanket advice, you ask a specific question of the card. Keep this question in mind while you shuffle the cards, and be ready for the answer.

Three-Card
Past-Present-Future Spread

This is a straightforward snapshot approach to a spread. Think of a par-ticular situation or question you'd like insight on, or just ask the cards for their take on what patterns need a check-in. Shuffle, then pull three cards and place them in front of you, from left to right.

1: past energy of the given situation.
2: present circumstances.
3: future, and possible things to come.

The Celtic Cross

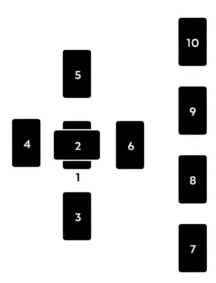

One of the most popular, enduring spreads, largely because it came in the instructional manual for the Rider-Waite-Smith deck. It's also fairly simple and straightforward.

1: The self, and the current situation.
2: What's getting in the way.
3: The unconscious energy affecting the situation.
4: The past.
5: Present circumstances.
6: The future.
7: The best approach.
8: People/influences in your life.
9: Hopes and fears.
10: The outcome.

Eleven-Card Motherpeace Spread

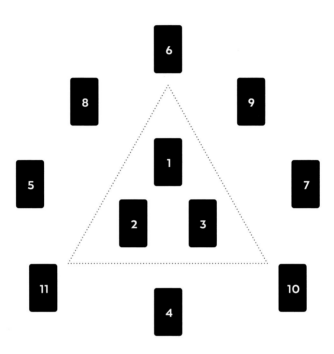

This spread's useful for getting the big picture, including the full nitty-gritty details. It's a deceptively simple twist on the Celtic Cross (page 32) but gives many subtle, complex, new layers to explore in our inner and outer lives. It was created by Vicki Noble, Karen Vogel, and Jonathan Tenney for the Motherpeace deck workbook, something I discovered over thirty years ago. Since then, it's become one of my go-to spreads for a succinct inner- and overview.

The first three cards of the spread represent the heart of the matter and form a triangle shape at the middle of the spread.

1: Your essence and where you're at currently, whether you know it or not.
2: The question being asked and what's currently on your mind.

3: The crossing card, the thing that's creating tension or desire. It points out the energy that is causing concern or has your attention. It needn't be negative.

The next four cards create a diamond shape around the heart of the matter.

4: What's going on in the root consciousness, or unconscious desires and lessons in play. This position often points to the real issue at hand, not just what is triggering it. These often subconsciously held issues and belief patterns from the past can be released and/or modified.
5: Conscious energy in or out. Your personality, external frequency.
6: The recent past: energy moving out of your life that has influenced current circumstances or mental/emotional state.
7: The immediate future: what's coming up if you continue along the current course of action.

The next four cards form a square pattern and show the fixed ideas your foundation is built upon and what energy resides there.

8: Self-identity: how you see yourself currently. This card differs from the first card in that this is your perception of you, which can match up or vary greatly from how the outside world receives your energy. A heavy card here can signify an overly critical nature.
9: Hopes and fears: we often put so much thought into low-vibration fear-based thoughts that the universe can receive them as a prayer, as if we're hoping for the thing we dread the most. It's tough to manifest what we really hope for if only negative thoughts are stretching out and eating up mental space and time.
10: Someone around you: this is the energy of another person (or people) around you who is affecting the current situation.
11: Outcome: this is a possible outcome based on the current path, or the story laid out. If you get a major card here, it carries more weight, and means things will probably go that way. If there's no Major Arcana card in this position, you can pull up to three more cards to clarify or see of a major card comes up. If one does not, it could mean the situation is unclear.

Let's look at some of this spread's shape patterns in more detail.

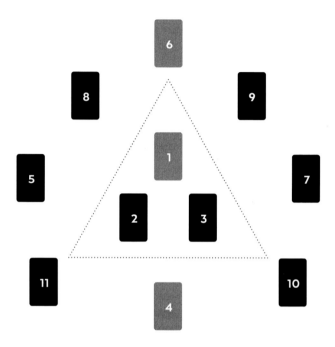

THE LINEAR LINE: Cards 6, 1, and 4 form a straight line, and combined, they represent the energy you're currently carrying from head to toes: Card 4, the root consciousness for what's buried deep; card 1, how you're currently thinking; and card 6, the conscious energy going in or out. Do these three cards together present clues to how you're vibrating? Do you see a through line of any particular suit or number patterns emerging?

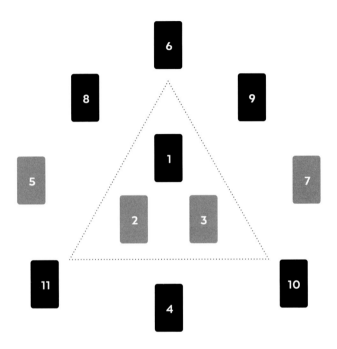

THE NORTH-SOUTH AXIS: Now look at card 5, the past; card 2, your present; card 3, the cross-current card; and card 7, the near upcoming future. This pattern runs left to right on the horizontal axis across the middle of your spread. Note any patterns or lack thereof: this axis shows what kind of energy is moving out of and coming into your life.

Ten-Card Relationship Snapshot Spread

Relationship readings are a way to check in energetically without disrespecting someone's boundaries, texting, or social media stalking. You can strengthen a psychic connection with another person by engaging through your spirit connection.

If you do this spread or others like it constantly, it can become energetically draining to you and the person you have eyes on. This can repel, rather than attract, your intended. Obsessively throwing cards over and over does not give you the time needed to digest the information you've received. Use your tarot with integrity—don't be an energy vampire.

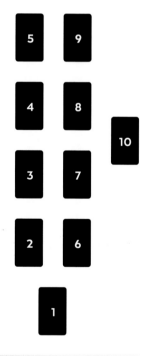

1: Where the dynamic is at currently.
2: Where your head is.
3: Where your heart is.
4: What energy you're putting out to the other party.
5: What you really think about the situation.
6: Where the other person's head is.
7: Where the other person's heart is.
8: What energy the other party is putting out to you.
9: What the other person really thinks about the situation.
10: The outcome or where things are headed.

If a Major Arcana doesn't land in position 10, the outcome is still developing, and you can pull two or three clarifying cards as needed.

True Heart Tarot Five-Card Insight Spread

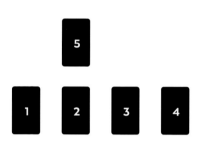

I developed this spread for myself years ago as a quick and easy way to gain insight into any given situation. You can use just the Major Arcana or the whole deck. This is an ideal spread to pull from only the Major Arcana cards, especially if the stakes of your query are high.

Sometimes the card that lands in the first position of this spread, representing what you desire, may seem off base with what you're consciously desiring. When this happens, continue laying out the spread, and sit with the reading or step away. Do the dishes or a repetitive task and let your thoughts see if they can connect any dots. When you come back and view the spread through fresh eyes, you might be surprised by new revelations.

If you're unsure what the cards are saying, pull one or two clarifying cards, if you like. Tarot has a way of ferreting out our underlying subconscious desires, if you're willing to listen. Throwing another spread right away or pulling too many extra cards can dilute the message.

1: What you desire
2: Will you get it?
3: Is this desire in alignment with your higher self?
4: If attained, will this desire sustain?
5: Where your energy should be focused.

Sample True Heart Tarot Insight Spread

This is a reading done for a friend of mine, Kara, who's up for a big movie. She's been working in a small part on a television show, but has long admired the director's films, so the entire project would be a dream come true. She's been put on tape for the role a few times, which is a good sign, but she is nervous regarding her chances. She chose five cards from my facedown shuffled deck.

1: 4 of Wands

This card represents celebrations, building a solid foundation and achieving milestones. This shows how much getting the part would mean to her.

2: 3 of Cups

This card is also upbeat, social, and celebratory, but a little more transitory, the way movie sets can be. This bodes well for her chances, to my intuition.

3: Princess of Wands

The job, if attained, will be stimulating, creatively charged, and probably a total rush.

4: Prince of Discs

It might sustain financially beyond this one job. It's a great opportunity, and my intuition says if she books it and shines, a chance meeting with someone on set may result in more work and more cash.

5: 2 of Cups

This project seems like a great fit. The 2 of Cups represents a union with something you greatly desire.

Despite the lack of Major Arcana in Kara's spread, which herald bigger shifts and a more definitive outcome, this was a very positive reading. As it stands, with the 2 of Cups hovering above, it feels like the cards are saying to keep focused on the thing you love, which in this case is the job.

Even before she left my house, an email came in that the director of the project wanted to meet with her. Two weeks later, she booked the role.

Final Thoughts on Spreads

This is but a smattering of the vast multitude of spreads available in books and online. Play around with as many as you can find until you land on a few you love. After you're beyond the basics of reading tarot, feel free to modify and create your own spreads. You can use these as a springboard to other spreads to map out your design.

Whether reading for yourself or others, interpreting spreads can be a highly subjective endeavor, which is why the best readers are cognizant of the need to sidestep egotistic desires for a certain outcome. Remaining objective is easier when you take your time and look for the clues in the cards pulled. Seasoned pros may be able to take a cursory glance at a complicated spread and be spot on in their reading of it. If you're new to tarot and energy work, trying to leapfrog forward robs you of an opportunity to hone your intuition.

Spreads unveil mysteries when you take the time to connect the dots. Meditating on a spread helps you develop your understanding of cards' relationships to one another and awakens your connection to your intuition. When you start to get little whispers of information, pay attention and listen up. Write them down to chart your progression, and trust your inner voice.

If there are Court cards in your reading, note if they're facing, or "interacting," with other people cards. In a relationship spread full of Sword cards, you might notice the figures and the various cards are all turned away from one another, mirroring the message of other cards pulled.

Paying attention to the dominant suit and its energy in a spread gives a major tip as to which direction to take the reading. For example, you may ask about work and receive mostly upbeat Cups cards. Either you're really loving your job, or the reading now becomes about your love life. This is where your gut reaction and intuition will guide you, if you trust it. Tarot readings can cheer you on or call you out—either way, it's information your higher self wants to receive.

THE
MAJOR
ARCANA

0 The Fool

HIGH VIBE · Beginnings, risk, naïveté, impulse, freedom, instinct, opportunity

LOW VIBE · Recklessness, initiation, blind eye, self-centeredness, fear of change, delusion

Every hero's journey begins with a first step. The Fool is one of the few Major Arcana cards traditionally portrayed with a figure in motion. This eternal soul is more curious about the journey than the actual destination. The Fool views the world with a sense of childlike wonder. Infinite possibilities exist.

In one hand, they hold a white flower, symbolizing innocence; in the other, a staff, symbolizing energy. Notice how light the pack on The Fool's staff is. They are unfettered by the trappings of failure or success.

The Fool is shown with their trusted dog, yapping at their side. Use your intuition to decide if the dog is barking encouragement or caution. No matter; The Fool heeds no warning! Like a child, they can only view the world through the prism of themselves.

Modern society would be quick to disregard the archetypal Fool, but remember who had the king's ear at court; every fool in Shakespeare was the smartest character onstage; and the Roman emperor Claudius played the fool and outlived most of his relatives, including his nephew, the notorious Caligula.

Beginnings often mean endings; The Fool may connote a release from people, places, and things weighing your energy down. Take a deep breath in and visualize your perfect future. For some, you might need to quiet your mind and leap, eyes wide shut, into your future. Follow your impulses; adventure awaits!

In relationship dynamics, you may be filled with excitement and joy over a new person, place, or thing that's entered your sphere. There's a transitory nature to The Fool; they can come and go. For singles, an energetic, lighthearted vibe can attract suitors. This is the time to shake up your world and get back on the dating scene—the possibilities are endless.

In professional life, luck, fortune, and new opportunities should be presenting themselves. If you're a newbie, be on the lookout for ways to climb the ladder. You can impress the higher-ups with your drive and determination to succeed. Stay positive, and chances are a risk will pay off. Sometimes The Fool card is pulled when someone feels swamped by new responsibilities. If this is you, keep an eye out for possible mentors who can help you explore what your best options are.

IF PULLED IN LOW VIBE · When you refuse to acknowledge what's right in front of your face, when you're in your ego, you are the embodiment of the low-vibration Fool.

You may have wandered too far off-path and need to take heed of a blinking caution sign. Keep your feet planted on terra firma, lest a detour leave you stranded. Don't bet the farm or take unnecessary risks. Burying your head, delaying decisions, and ignoring the details can come back to haunt you. It's time to approach life with more maturity.

Selfish, unreliable, or impractical partners in professional life or romance may be throwing you off balance. Weigh your options and keep it light before signing on long-term. This is your chance to follow your dreams; don't let anyone steal your sunshine.

· · · · · ·

When I booked my first studio movie and prepared to move out to the West Coast, I packed up my rent-controlled steal of an apartment in New York and pulled a few cards before tucking my tarot decks in my carry-on bag: The Fool, 9 of Swords, and The Chariot. The Fool was saying to take a risk and leap into a new adventure. My worry and fear about moving, represented by the 9 of Swords, were just that—fear and worry, not reality. And The Chariot, a card of victory on the worldly plane, was in the future position.

California is earthquake country, terra not-so-firma. For a West Coast newbie, this volatile core energy felt like a conduit magnifying my intuition. Tarot was grounding for me in those early days.

After shooting my first studio film (*CB4*, which Chris Rock cast me in as the naive, Lenny Kravitz–loving boho Delilah), there was no more acting work to be found. Heroin chic was in vogue, and I was a far way off from the pale, white-skinned somnambulistic waifs who made up the bulk of Hollywood actresses. I was an East Village-y, black-clad brown dot in a very bright and white new land, without a rule book. I'd moved my entire life across the country on two weeks' notice, without any thought to what would happen next.

My bills were paid by residuals and the graces of the unemployment gods, the patron saints of all actors, so I was lucky enough not to need a "job-job." Even with that slight luxury, I was stuck in a sort of performer's malaise, from a lack of auditions and no structure.

Worst of all, my television died (this was pre-internet territory, dial-up at best). I was stuck in silence, sitting with my own boredom.

I brought out my slightly neglected tarot cards, choosing Motherpeace, a sweet and gentle round deck, and pulled The Hanged Man and Hierophant a few times. I tried another deck, but the message from all parties was clear: I was in a bit of a holding pattern.

That wasn't going to work for me. I wanted momentum! I needed to be moving forward at all times! I wanted to be in a flick everyone loved, like *Heathers*!

I could fix my telly, but I figured I might as well use my powers for good and get my focus on. I took the non-self-imposed work sabbatical to fine-tune my energy and vibrate a little higher. That manifested by getting deeper into my tarot cards, meditating, and studying any tarot books I could get my hands on. I kept copious notes, annotated with drawings, filling up many journals, and began developing a profound relationship with the cards and, in turn, myself.

While I still felt in stasis (The Hanged Man loomed large), my daily tarot practice became a tool of creation.

About nine months later, a friend told me about a movie I was perfect for called *The Craft*. After I read the script, I told her, "If anyone's going to be a little black witch in this town, it's me!"

I know the script for *The Craft* was attracted to me because of my enduring relationship to the cards and mystical studies. What if instead of going deeper with the tarot, I had gotten my TV fixed and waited around for auditions to trickle back in? Maybe I still would've somehow ended up booking *The Craft*—some parts are meant to be yours—but maybe my energy would have been off from lethargy and disengagement, defeated by the constant nos an actor endures. Would my vibration have matched my character, Rochelle? Thank goodness I'll never have to know.

Today's burgeoning spiritualists may have had their first intro to tarot while watching *The Craft*. In 1996, the Sony Pictures cult film debuted at number one at the box office, and stayed there until *Mission: Impossible* crushed us two weeks later. Somehow, the little witchy flick that could has endured. To this day, I'm routinely offered free hemp bracelets and a spot in the coven by random teens at airports the world over.

The Fool can make all the plans they want, but until they begin taking steps, the path will remain uncertain.

1 The Magician

HIGH VIBE · **Transformation, creativity, action, will, strength, expertise, intellect, skill, confidence, discipline, charisma**

LOW VIBE · **Deceit, stagnation, lack of focus, manipulation, powerlessness, delusion, dishonesty**

The Fool started with nothing; they leapt off a cliff, and whatever their journey, they have matured in their knowledge. They transformed into The Magician.

The Magician holds a wand toward the sky, representing thought; you can almost hear them pronounce, "So it is above, as it is below." The other hand points to the earth, replete with living flora, representing thought manifested on the physical plane. The Magician transforms thoughts into reality through a combination of action, intellect, and creativity.

The Magician is surrounded by each of the four suits of the tarot; they have all the tools at their disposal, and now they must galvanize their skills. It's up to The Magician to put in the requisite 10,000 hours it takes to gain mastery of any skill. Above The Magician's head is the infinity symbol, signifying the infinite possibilities at their disposal.

Having stumbled a few times, The Magician has gained a larger perspective and is more tactical than the naive Fool. When you pull The Magician, the tarot is telling you to remove your rose-colored glasses, to see the world beyond your own perspective. Develop your innate talents to move forward; everything is laid out in front of you.

The Magician acts on their thoughts to create the life they desire. They are all action, struck by inspiration, a new vision. This card is a reminder to make the most of opportunities and synthesize them into tangible results. Create your own destiny. Take the next step on your journey, and become The Magician.

If you receive The Magician in a reading, in the present or future position, make the most of an exciting opportunity. It will move you closer to your goals and toward integrating the different sides of yourself. A new clarity and the thrill of self-discovery make this a heady time. Your clever mind is working overtime. Keep focused, and magic can happen.

In relationship dynamics, The Magician may signify a powerful attraction to a mysterious stranger, or a renewed spark and deeper level of connection to a current partner. Be prepared for anything with this fascinating character, and communicate your dating needs, or you might end up bedazzled by smoke and mirrors. Single people should get ready to mingle: potential lovers will find you magnetic.

In professional life, you're no longer relying solely on luck or the kindness of strangers: you're creating own destiny. You're one to watch, coming up with innovative ideas that just work and clever ways to implement them. Keep up the hard work! If you've started or plan to start a new venture, The Magician says the timing is right.

IF PULLED IN LOW VIBE · The Magician can manifest as a charismatic, manipulative person, stuck in hubris. Ask yourself, are you using your talents for good, or is ego controlling your current actions? Are you being unscrupulous in your dealings?

The Magician may represent someone in your life who is pulling the wool over your eyes. Never forget that you hold great power within; activate your personal alchemy.

For some, energy feels off, and it's impossible to manifest. Take stock of where you invest your time. Let go of distractions that are pulling you off your path. It's hard to succeed if you're not trying. Negative thought patterns, anxiety, or a loss of faith in yourself should be addressed. It's time for action and a move forward with plans and goals. This is your sign: turn yourself back on.

······

When I was a sophomore at NYU, I attended a scene night my then boyfriend was performing in at Tisch, NYU's art school.

The class performed their scenes proficiently. They were feeling themselves out onstage, still putting together their bag of acting tricks. I watched them, full of my low vibration envy; I was mad I was not onstage with them. I'd entered NYU with a journalism slant, and basically sat in typing classes daydreaming of acting someday.

Tisch was mainly made up of white, upper-middle-class-to-rich students. Hothouse flowers, given every advantage, from summers at Interlochen Arts Academy to trips studying theater history in places that birthed the arts. These kids were bred to succeed. I was brown-skinned and unmonied; I'd have to work twice as hard just to get the same chances.

I clapped after my boyfriend's scene, though its pacing was off. Later I found out he'd slept with his male scene partner that week, not my last college liaison to come out as beyond gay. At the time I didn't have the confidence to think I deserved or could attract real love.

Despite all this, I was grateful to be in that class that day. A teen-aged Philip Seymour Hoffman (pre–Academy Award) performed a John

Patrick Shanley scene so electric, I knew I was witnessing the birth of a supernova. He'd moved past illusion and into actual magic, utilizing the energy of the suits; he was clear of mind (Swords), full of fire (Wands), grounded in reality (Discs), and lovingly attentive to the author's intentions for the scene (Cups). The tools at his disposal were wielded with confidence.

The audience, including myself, was jolted awake, inspired by the raw talent on display and more than a little embarrassed by our own lack thereof. I felt terrible for the students who had to follow him, their scenes made static by the palpable realization that they were not as naturally gifted as their high school theater teachers had led them to believe.

In that moment, I thought of The Magician card. The fiery energy shook me out of my self-pity and into my future. Fear and loathing in Rachel-land were holding me back from pursuing my own dreams full force. I was afraid to get up and perform, afraid to make a fool of myself. It hit me that to be an actor meant to be fearless, unafraid to take risks. It was not about what you were saying onstage; it was about what you were feeling.

I decided I wanted to transfer to one of Tisch's acting programs, and prepared an audition. Medium story short, I did not get in. I sat and cried a river of tears that swelled my eyes shut for all to see at Loeb Student Center off Washington Square Park. My dreams were broken into too many pieces to fathom gathering up and Frankenstein-ing them back together. Obviously, I would never be an actor, I thought, defeated. I'd died, and the identity-less liminal state I found myself in was to be my eternal purgatory.

I went through the requisite beating-myself-up period for probably too long. And then I thought about what most professional actors endured. The sheer number odds in booking roles would mean a constant cycle of rejection with a smattering of wins. A relentless phoenix to the flame and back again, hope and faith that tomorrow was another opportunity to shine. I also had to admit I'd let my nerves get the best of me. Some nerves are healthy; too much meant I wasn't prepared enough and/or had to tackle my anxiety.

Tenacity can overcome deficits, when focused. My singular certainty that I was supposed to be an actor forced me to consider a new approach, one with a more practical slant. I would need to study; I would need to apprentice and learn. I knew if I did this, nothing could stop me from one day earning the right to sit on a set. Luckily, baby me had desire, tenacity, some talent, ego, and grit working for her. Was it a mistake that I didn't get in? No; that failure was the catalyst for tremendous personal transformation. It was the start of dedicating myself to learning a craft, rather than daydreaming about being on a film set. I enrolled in acting classes at HB Studio, a small space run by the husband of the late, great acting teacher Uta Hagen. Tisch students looked down their noses at HB, but there I was, lucky enough to study with Earle Hyman for Shakespeare and many great stage and film actors, who taught classes in between gigs.

All of us are magical. When we recognize our own strengths and hone them, we are The Magician personified.

2 The High Priestess

HIGH VIBE · Intuition, knowledge, wisdom, thoughtfulness, esoteric mysteries, connection to higher self, psychic visions

LOW VIBE · Disconnection, isolation, loneliness, lack of faith, materialism, confusion

The High Priestess signifies our inner intuition as well as our psychic connection to the esoteric world, God (as you understand them), and the unknown. In a sense, they are the feminine spiritual equivalent to The Hierophant, though less vocal and dogmatic in their approach.

The High Priestess is portrayed as a bit serious, austere, and regal. They hold a partially obscured book of wisdom, and are wise enough to know when to be quiet and not give away all their secrets. Beneath them is a crescent moon, signifying the subconscious mind. They are attuned to the spiritual guidance within and around them, unraveling life's mysteries. Uncovering and processing information not fully comprehended by others is their specialty.

The High Priestess is a reminder to trust your inner intuition and pay attention to your premonitions. If you've pulled this card, go deep into the mystery of you and learn to discern your higher self's inner voice from the anxious noise of the lower self. The veil between reality and projection is lifting. The spiritual self in tune with intuition teaches us the power of knowing when not to reveal too much or push too hard; The High Priestess asks us to recognize and use our specific unique gifts to access the witchy person within.

You might be studying with a spiritual mentor or advisor whose ideas rock your world, or undertaking the process on your own. Either way, your passion for life is engaged, your intuition opening. Some may find they're enjoying spending more time with themselves. Epiphanies and insights may seize you moment by moment. Others around you may not be experiencing the same phenomenon, leaving you feeling isolated. Some lessons are to be explored alone. Tracking your thoughts through journal work will allow you to apply them to real-life situations.

In relationship dynamics, you may feel connected to loved ones, and have an intuitive knowing of their needs. There can be a desexualized, buttoned-up feel to the High Priestess, but what they do behind closed doors is between them and their partner. Some couples may need temporary space, and singles may decide to take a break from dating for a short time to refocus on themselves.

In professional life, keep cool, calm, and collected in appearance and thought. When confusion and chaos erupt, you might be the one to shed important light on the situation at hand. Be cognizant of timing and speaking with integrity. Your word should be impeccable for progress to ramp up. Base actions on knowledge rather than raw emotions.

IF PULLED IN LOW VIBE · Spending time by yourself is important, but when it turns to isolation and loneliness, broaden your perspective. You may feel a lack of faith, dissatisfaction, or isolation with others. Mental confusion can cause anxiety and depression. Sexual repression and a controlling nature may cause tension with others. Break out of the normal rituals and traditions: your higher self is waiting to be engaged.

. . . . . .

The High Priestess is one of my favorite cards, though I had trouble connecting to them in my early years, despite my being a very good Scorpio secret keeper and generally intuitive person. Back then, the High Priestess's austere nature, serious expression, and ability to keep their mouth shut collided with my natural exuberance and propensity to be outspoken. Looking back, it's quite clear I lacked the maturity to comprehend their depth.

Oddly enough, a solitary afternoon of binging far too many *Doctor Who* episodes gave some insight and opened up a few of The High Priestess's mysteries to me. The High Priestess is the ultimate Time Lord, for they know everything about the past, present, and far-flung future, and discern when and when not to announce their arrival and display their particular skill set. Unlike my then self, they knew better than to spill their truths before letting others expose who they are and what they are after.

Like The High Priestess, we all have the ability to travel through time, though we tend to do this mentally, not on the cellular level like Doctor Who. Mere mortals can get stuck in reliving the past on a loop. Our thoughts are consumed by things that have already happened, resulting in a state of depression. Anxiety is often a projection of what could go wrong in the present and in the future. Both are time-travel-y trips; it's easy to get waylaid by regret and despair or become paralyzed by fear of what's to come. Drowning in the victimhood of past foibles can veer into self-indulgence and herald a narcissistic streak. Reflecting on the past to gain insight is a good thing, but self-analyzing is very different from self-focusing.

I began to see The High Priestess less as a buttoned-up, taciturn schoolmarm and more as a person with a full and vibrant life, the details of which they chose to keep close to the vest, secreted away until the worthy approached. I respected and aspired to be a woman who trusted my intuition enough to know I didn't need to broadcast my many talents, correct others when they were wrong, or be what the kids call "prove-y."

The High Priestess encouraged me to embrace my intuitive, bordering on slightly psychic, nature. Despite my "hermit at home, loquacious out in public" disposition, I'd been actively censoring psychic hits because my observations seemed to make others uneasy and I was starting to feel like Cassandra from Greek mythology. That needed to change.

The issue was not my insights, but my delivery. I needed to become more aware of when and with whom I shared the bits of knowledge I pulled from the ether. I seemed to have a knack for saying things and asking people the exact questions that pushed their buttons. I'd always thought of this as simply my ability to pick up the vibe in the air, but hadn't quite understood how unnecessary it was to point it out sometimes. It was time to learn how to be High Priestess quiet, while utilizing my inner knowing. The hat trick for me would be mastering how not to get stuck in the past or wander too far into the future without a guide rope to get me back to the present.

One day in the middle of a Santa Monica Whole Foods dripping with see-through-yoga-pants-wearing starlets, I stood debating which fresh prepackaged food would save me from my own dreadful cooking when a voice that sounded like the rustling of leaves whispered, *Don't take the first samosa*. Huh, I thought, and grabbed the first samosa anyway, only to discover when I got home that there was a bug in it. My own internal voice of anxiety had been drowning out my intuition.

It was up to me to quietly go about the work of building a better, more grounded, and connected High Priestess Rachel 2.0, who could be more intuitive and more psychically connected to the world.

An apprenticeship under the tutelage of The High Priestess would take time, as would deracinating my emotions from deeply ingrained patterns. One method I found helpful was to explore and determine my "cool-off point." In other words, exactly how much time did it actually take for me to simmer down and think logically when dealt a blow in any given circumstance?

This meant allowing space and time to process my agita on my own or with a therapist, before reacting out on others. Calling friends and forcing them to live inside my spinning head was, in essence, asking them to experience my pain. I learned the power of silence, the gift of patience, and how to finally listen to my higher self, the one who seeks the guidance of The High Priestess before reacting.

3 The Empress

HIGH VIBE · **Sensuality, beauty, joy, fertility, love, fulfillment, pregnancy, sexuality, creativity**

LOW VIBE · **Emotional imbalance, jealousy, infertility, scarcity, unhappiness**

The Empress represents our connection to the divine feminine, the seat of our emotional, physical, and sexual power. They are the lover, the mother, the child, the creator, the goddess, and the destroyer.

The archetype for The Empress is a person who expresses their love and interest in others through creativity, collaborative arts, and sensual delights. This is an opportune moment to explore what love means, while connecting to the power of your passion. Learning to wield these gifts consciously is a paradigm shift that can usher in abundance and prosperity. This can be a period of fertile manifestation. The sparkly, effervescent energy and earthy seductiveness you carry will likely be a magnet to others; thoughtfully discern whom you let bathe in your sunshine.

The Empress reminds us to let love guide, whether it's love of self or of others. In a reading, The Empress may represent a maternal figure or friend who knows just when to lend support or offer a hug. The Empress is nurturing and hands-on, doting on their children and partner.

In relationship dynamics, The Empress is fully invested in the emotional well-being of others and offers encouragement and solace when needed. For some, a passionate, emotionally available partner or friend has you feeling loved, nurtured, and appreciated. Others may be opening up to dating again after a period of emotional shutdown. Long-term couples may reinvigorate their partnership and sex life. If single, imagine the kind of person who would fulfill you, tune into your love frequency, and remain open to opportunities. The Empress is a symbol of fertility and can indicate a possible pregnancy or additions to the family.

In professional life, abundant opportunities are available or will present themselves soon. Set up an altar or use a vision board to manifest and connect with your intuition. You can advance when you transform the prism through which you view the world. Creative teaching methods and intuitive guidance foster a feeling of belonging.

IF PULLED IN LOW VIBE · The Empress in a low vibe can represent a smothering parent, friend, or lover, drowning themselves and others in negative thoughts and behaviors. Suppressing emotions may cause you to shut down or react explosively toward others. Confusion, depression, anxiety, sexual dysfunction, and/or self-involved thinking can present as a victim mentality. Some may be using sexuality as a weapon or as their only means of connection. Attune to your higher self and release stagnant emotions blocking energy and creativity. Open up to the plethora of opportunities, connections, and love currently around you.

. . . . . .

A few years ago, my sister made an offhand comment about the time my older brother and I were in foster care. I sat up, curious. "I thought . . . that's just the time we lived with those other people . . ."

My sister rolled her eyes. "Yeah, Rachel, that's what foster care is."

That's how, as an adult, I realized that maybe living "with other people" had more to do with shaping me than I'd given credit, though I was lucky that Oma and Opa, as we called them, were kindly people and provided more stability than I'd ever know again in my childhood. My memories of that time are scattered, though I recall being small, annoyed, and anxious that other children were constantly moving in and out of *my* room.

Memories of my mother from that time remain behind a Gaussian filter: a half-formed daydream of a hand, a swish of wigged hair, a moon-sized medallion around a neck, a symphony of beads clacking as she walked away, all velvet and hot pants, insecurity, ambition, and beauty bundled in an early-seventies "manic pixie black girl" confection. I imagined she was a supermodel who traveled for work, and that's why I lived with other people.

My father once said that my problem was I "didn't get enough time on [my] mother's tit." Crassly put, but probably not wholly untrue.

While in foster care, my brother and I would sometimes visit our biological mother. On those infrequent trips, my mother would immediately liberate my hair from the two plaits I wore on the daily and let it loose to hang long and free, blowing in the breeze. She'd dress me in outfits matching her own, made from Indian hippie tapestries.

My Jewish father married another black woman after my mother, something that endlessly confused my friends. My brother and I left foster care and moved in with them. My stepmom was tall and beautiful, but she had not been raised in an affectionate home, and she wasn't a hugger. The lack of touch was not personal, but I took it personally. I felt she saw my longing for my mother as a rejection of her, and her and my father's condemnation of my mother left me feeling embarrassed and ashamed to love someone who'd rejected me.

My brother and I had our last great hurrah with our birth mother when I was eight years old. She was moving out to the West Coast with her new husband, a long-haired rock musician. We met them in the Rockies and road-tripped out to California. It was a trip filled with ups and downs, to put it mildly. Our stepfather was driving a van loaded with Mexican pottery, which was definitely/probably/allegedly full of shitty Mexican weed. His band opened for Loggins and Messina. I'm embarrassed to admit how puffed up with ego my baby self was, how special I felt to be with my mother, dressed in matching dashikis as we cut the line so she could flash her backstage pass. Such a boss power move.

Eventually our road trip ended at a small rented San Fernando Valley house, where my brother and I slept on pallets on the floor, my anxiety building at both the general instability and the light show sparking from the electrical outlet by my head at night. During the day I'd routinely walk in circles around the block, hoping a Hollywood agent would discover me.

I had rotating crushes on my stepfather's bandmates and a new neighbor who paid me a quarter to walk his dog. But in all of this, what stood out is how much I wanted to be the center of my mother's universe. This is not abnormal for kids, but can be dangerous if carried into adulthood. This dynamic was learned from the atmosphere in my father's house, where affection tended to be mercurial and only bestowed on one child at a time. It meant my brother and I were voracious pits of need, desperate for motherly affection, which she showered on us when we scored time with her. My stepfather found this tedious enough to denigrate it. Seeing how we were with her, he cracked, "Are you guys gonna follow her into the bathroom and wipe her ass?"

My mother loved us, of this I have no doubt. But we were the last pieces of a life she'd been pushed out of, and we began to hear from her less and less. I wouldn't spend time with her again until I was fifteen and traveled out to Los Angeles to visit her. She picked me up and whisked me off to an after-hours nightclub I was far too young to patronize. "Oh, by the way, everyone here in Cali thinks I'm twenty-six, not forty. I told them you're my sister, so don't call me Mom."

Despite this reddish flag, I thought moving into her small one-bedroom off Beachwood Canyon was a good idea. I was going to realize my dream of becoming an actor! So, after my junior year of high school,

I moved—nay, *marched*—out of my dad's house in upstate New York. My plan was to stay with my aunt and uncle on Long Island for two weeks, until my mother sent me a ticket back to Los Angeles.

Two weeks stretched into three, then four. Finally, at week six, my uncle told me what time it was. "Your mom says it's not a good idea for you to come out, and maybe you should consider going back to your dad's."

I was gutted; it felt like a sucker punch. I thought I'd forever left behind my dad's house in upstate New York, and all its miserable snow and racism. And my mother hadn't even had the nerve to tell me herself? I felt tethered to my child self, who was already aware that her only mission was to grow up and get out.

Unfortunately, this would begin a long pattern of mistrust and miscommunication between my birth mother and me. I wouldn't see her again till my thirtieth birthday; on the same day, I was shooting a commercial and taking a meeting with Steven Spielberg. Her arrival was an unhelpful distraction.

Though she is the person who showed me what love is, my mother is also responsible for how I've most often dealt with it: by encasing my heart and hiding my feelings.

Years later, when my father died, my stepmother put her hand on my shoulder and said, "I'm sorry I wasn't more loving." Here was the woman who'd raised me, sent me a few bucks when I needed it, and put up with my bullshit. While not overly affectionate, she'd provided me with something priceless: stability. Eventually she learned to hug on cue, as I have, too, and now when we end our conversations she says, "I love you," something I still struggle to articulate even when I feel it. It's something I'm working on, and with the guidance of The Empress, something I hope to overcome.

4 The Emperor

HIGH VIBE · Control, security, power, force, stubbornness, authority, intellect, stability, rigidity, discipline, structure, logic

LOW VIBE · Immaturity, passivity, fear, cruelty, control issues, cowardice, unmotivated, blunt-force victimhood, loose cannon

The Emperor represents a strong-willed individual who conquers with intellect, might, and practiced skill. This commanding, action-oriented archetype with an eye for detail offers wise counsel and guidance as easily as tough, disciplinary justice, when needed.

If you pull The Emperor, instinct, intelligence, drive, and dedication may have landed you a recent hard-won success. If that's not the case, use this time to actively pursue what you desire and examine how and where your energy and focus are divided. Well-thought-out, decisive action is called for. This is no time for excuses; trying to win with sentiment is futile. A logical mind will move you forward.

You may need to defend your honor or end a pattern of other people walking over you. Trust you've got the acumen to solidify a foundation for future success.

In relationship dynamics, an assertive, intelligent, clever personality who likes things their way may have entered your life. Fair and not overly emotional, The Emperor can tend to run their family and/or relationships like a business. This might not create a warm and fuzzy dynamic, but the solid support offered is unparalleled. You'll feel safe, protected, and loved by the Emperor archetype. They'll push you to be your best and come to your aid when deemed fit.

In professional life, The Emperor can be an authority figure who sets the rules. Speak up and base decisions on facts. Your natural charisma makes you a born leader; take others' opinions into consideration before acting, and they'll follow you willingly. If your boss is the demanding sort, they'll be impressed by those who mirror their own never-ending drive and ambition.

IF PULLED IN LOW VIBE · Heavy is the head that wears the crown. How will you wield your power?

Issues of control can arise when The Emperor feels underappreciated. They may become aloof and judgmental, cutting others off without warning. Claim your power while staying open to the needs of others. Overbearing, aloof, or defensive behavior may be causing tension and setbacks. Hubris and control issues can be a cover for low self-esteem, fear of failure, depression, or anxiety. You may be driving away fertile opportunities. It's time to loosen the reins and seize your victory.

······

In 1990, I was living in the East Village and trying to make it as an actress. I'd just finished a lead role in an indie film and was picking up small parts on soaps, but my steady source of income was bartending at a Mexican spot called Caliente Cab on Waverly Place. I was the only black employee they had, and it wasn't working out. A reggae club had opened up next door, and suddenly Caliente Cab decided it needed a "dress code," meaning sneakers weren't permitted. I could see the writing on the wall when my schedule started including fewer and fewer shifts, and then zero shifts. They didn't want black—ahem, "sneaker-wearing"—patrons, and they didn't want a black bartender. I wish I could say I sued them, but those were different times. It was just the way it was.

A friend told me there was an audition for stand-ins on *The Cosby Show*. It's an essential job, but for my younger, ambitious self, it wasn't attractive. "Pass," I said. "I want on-camera work, and stand-ins are basically glorified extras."

"It's on the freaking *The Cosby Show*, you dummy," she said. "The number one show in the world! Imagine all the people you could meet on a set like that who could hire you later. Just go."

She was right. More important, I needed a job. I hopped on the subway in a borrowed vintage dress and headed for downtown Astoria, Queens, with its row houses, flowered hedges, and backyards. When I got to the studio, there was already a serious line of people wrapped around it, all of whom looked pretty much like me. Some were dancing and singing show tunes, *Fame*-style, and all of them were ready for their moment. Not my thing. Living in an NYU dorm with Sondheim fanatics had ruined all that for me. I hooked up my Walkman to a Hazel O'Connor punk mix and hunkered down for what promised to be a righteous wait.

Eventually, we were herded into groups of five and led down a long hallway to meet Ann, the stage manager of the show, and her assistant director, Maynard. There was a quick interview, a headshot check, and a sentence or two apiece. It was like group speed dating. When it was my turn, Maynard said, "Oh, that's a Lisa Bonet dress."

Without thinking, I shot back, "Oh no, this is a Rachel True dress."

"Who's Rachel True?"

"I am." I handed him my headshot, well aware that I was wasting my time.

When I got home, there was a message from Maynard on my machine; I'd gotten the thumbs-up. I knew it wasn't a killer job or anything, but it was steady pay, and as dismissive as I initially felt about the gig, I was thrilled to be associated with such an iconic show.

Here, live and in person, were all the people America couldn't get enough of on Thursday nights. I actually hadn't seen many episodes—I didn't have a television—but I was well aware of who Theo, Rudy, Sabrina, Vanessa, and Denise Huxtable were. Lisa Bonet, who played Denise, was returning to the show after having left *A Different World* to marry Lenny Kravitz and have their baby, Zoë, who was six months old and nestled in a stroller nearby. They'd decided to give Denise a stepchild, Olivia, played by Raven-Symoné, and a husband, Martin, played by Joseph Phillips. The cast were chatting casually on the stage floor when in walked the man, the myth, The Emperor himself, Bill Cosby. He was chomping on a cigar, which turned the freezing air on the sound stage into a curious mixture of stale smoke and freon.

Bill, or Mr. Cosby, as most people referred to him, was a master at milking a comedy bit. Did he have a super-magnetic, powerful vibe? *Yes*. Did he have a weird undercurrent of something you couldn't put your finger on? *Definitely*. I wrote it off as my own envy and insecurity in the face of such power.

A stand-in's primary job is to act out the blocking, or movement, of the main characters for the technical run-through. This way, the actors get a break while the cameramen work out the shots. I would recite the lines of whichever Cosby kid I was standing in for: Vanessa (played by Tempestt Bledsoe) at first, and eventually Denise. These weren't performances; I was going through the motions of what other people got to act out. Stand-ins are game pieces, essentially, but it was great practice, and a chance to hone my comedy chops.

One of the other new stand-ins was a pretty, light-skinned girl who favored Lisa Bonet, and clearly had a personal relationship with Bill Cosby. He would come over and interact with her in a familiar way, and she would flirt with him. She sat apart from the rest of us to let us know her rank. After a few weeks, she was replaced by a new light-skinned girl, who happened to live in a condo on the same block as Mr. Cosby and had a dog that was the same breed as the dogs the star comedian raised and showed. I'm not *saying* she was a side chick, but

I guess I'm saying it *looked like* she was a side chick, and she wasn't dispelling that notion.

Eventually I landed speaking roles on the show, not the norm for stand-ins. Once I was a patient of Bill's, and in a couple of episodes I was a college friend of Theo's. Taking into account all we now know about the star's sexual criminality, I was lucky I always flew under his radar. Not that I had anything to worry about; I am a shade or two darker than a paper bag (ahem).

In the two and a half years I worked there, Camille Cosby, Bill's wife, never made an appearance in Queens. It was almost as if as if she didn't exist. And it didn't take long to notice the parade of women who came through as "special guests of Mr. Cosby" every week, without fail. He seemed to have a lot of lady friends. I never thought terribly much of it, because he was a powerful man and a lot of women flocked to him. The vibe he gave off around these women seemed paternal. It never occurred to me that any liaison would be anything but nonsexual, let alone nonconsensual.

My thoughts on the benign nature of these acquaintances shifted, however, during the series's last season, when one of Mr. Cosby's friends showed up on tape day looking visibly traumatized. She was normally a bright, vivacious girl, who'd visited set often as part of Bill's parade, before landing a small costarring role on the show. She'd been nervous all week, but now her hand shook as she held her script, and her eyes were noticeably downcast, avoiding Bill's gaze.

During a break, a few of us took her aside to find out what was wrong. In a broken, hushed tone, she recounted to us that Bill had requested she go to his house to run lines the night before. At first, I thought he'd just chewed her out for having a rough acting week. While she wasn't specific, she was shaking as she intoned that something more untoward had gone down. She'd been through something and was afraid to say what.

I could see her internal struggle: She could reveal what had happened, and potentially be banished from the kingdom of Cosby, maybe even fired on the spot. Or she could white-knuckle through the taping, which is what she did.

I remember thinking, *I'd never go to a man's house late at night unless I was ready to give it up.* The '90s were peak victim blaming. Truth is, when there is an imbalance of power, sometimes it is impossible to say no.

Back then, Bill Cosby's public image was laughter, family values, pudding pops! He was the archetypal representation of the high vibrations of The Emperor, a man who wields his power benevolently.

But now we see a man who struggled with his shadow side. He was hiding behind The Emperor's mask but secretly living in its low-vibration energy.

5 The Hierophant

HIGH VIBE · Spiritual authority, tradition, religion, marriage, commitment, corporate structures

LOW VIBE · Suppression, control, *lack* of control, dogmatic nature, conservatism

The Hierophant has an inherent traditional slant, representing structured authority, organized religion, government institutions, and conservative thinking. While The High Priestess has an intuitive, quiet knowing, The Hierophant boldly proclaims, "This is the true and right way to do things."

On The Hierophant card sits a religious figure. Are they resting on their laurels, propped up by dogma? Or could they lead you to the path to enlightenment? Two acolytes kneel in reverie; The Hierophant's keys to knowledge are just within reach.

Flanking The Hierophant stand pillars from the Temple of Solomon. These same pillars appear on The High Priestess card, but now their symbols and some of their meaning have been removed. The High Priestess is spirit; The Hierophant is the human conduit for spirit.

If The Hierophant comes up, you may be starting an apprenticeship or religious training, or dealing with marriage/divorce or any situation involving an authority figure who holds power and knowledge and by whose will you must abide. The Hierophant's rules and guidelines can either give structure or make you feel chained. This is an auspicious time to join a group with an ideology you support, or one that will open and expand your mind.

History is full of inventive people who challenged cultural norms and shaped our modern world, as well as those whose contributions came in a more traditional fashion. We are best able to serve our fellow man when we're living in our truth. Listen to your higher self and live an authentic life, even if that leads you away from the values you grew up with.

In relationship dynamics, some may be joyfully preparing for marriage or ceremonies of all design. Family obligations may take up your time and papers may need to be signed and notarized. If you've met someone new, take it slow and get to know them before rushing in, and you could build a solid foundation for a lasting relationship. For others, counseling, of the psychological or religious variety, should be considered to mend dynamics.

In professional life, you may have a great new mentor. Or you may be bristling over the actions of a person with authority over you. If so, get out of low vibe; learning to work within the system will give you the knowledge and freedom you seek in order to implement forward-thinking change. Consult with others to get the full picture before making any risky moves. Be respectful when seeking guidance, and you might gain a lifelong personal champion.

IF PULLED IN LOW VIBE · Conforming without thought lowers your vibration. You may be feeling constrained by societal norms or family pressures that your current beliefs no longer align with. Use intuition and inner fortitude to guide you to the right path. Occasionally, for some, a false prophet or guru has swept you up in an identity of groupthink. Discern what your own personal code of morals and ethics comprises. For some couples, rigidity has led to malaise. A shakeup of the status quo may be in order. Divorce or legal separation may be on the table, depending on how The Hierophant aligns with other cards in your spread.

. . . . . .

When I was eleven, my father and stepmother announced that we were moving out of the East Village and relocating to upstate New York. Having been raised on *Little House on the Prairie*, I'd assumed on some unconscious level that leaving Manhattan meant getting fitted for a bonnet, running through fields of flowers, and riding in horse-drawn buggies. Instead I'd emerged in a gray, snow-covered, financially depressed wasteland.

For a time, we had a family of blond born-again Christians living close by. They went to church five days a week, and during a sleepover at their house one night, I was "saved."

"Don't you want to be up in heaven, laughing at the heathens being burnt alive below?" the older sister asked.

"Sure . . ." Giddy superiority didn't sound very Christian to me, even at that young age, but I played along. I was an agnostic hedging my bets.

She clapped her hands enthusiastically, unable to contain her excitement. "It'll be like a party in heaven, while everyone suffers below!"

I spent the next month wondering when Jesus was coming back on "The Suffer Tour" to set everyone on fire. Hopefully there'd be some kind of advance notice. He never came. Eventually, I realized people can be led to believe just about anything.

Aside from my brother, I was the only black student in the entire K-12 school. On the first day, we lined up boy, girl, boy, girl, and none of the boys would stand next to me. Later, while I was trying to find my bus home, a kindergartener called me the N-word, and I still admire the restraint I displayed that day in not punting him to the moon.

Not long after the move, I took our dog, rather uninspiringly named Rover, for a walk to the country store and got very lost. I saw a man clearing brush from his yard and asked for directions. He pointed a shotgun at me, then my dog, and yelled at me to get away from his property. I was numb with shock and turned back toward my house. I never told my parents, but I dreamed of the sound of bullets for weeks.

As a high school junior, I got the highest SAT scores anyone at my otherwise all-white public high school had ever gotten. Despite this, the guidance counselor dismissed my desire to go to a good four-year school, suggesting community college might be a better fit. Later in the year, I scored 100 in English on the Regents, New York's state exam for high schoolers. The next day, I was pulled into an office and told my score had been lowered by two points because of some unknown error. Coincidentally, another student, whom I'd noticed crying the day before about her lower-than-expected results, suddenly had her exam marked higher. I got the message. My brown girl dreams were not as important as those of my peers; my black girl magic was too threatening. I understood I had to work within the rigid American structure and keep my head down until an opening appeared.

These small examples are de rigueur microaggressions, frankly. Some institutional traditions, like racism, give us no choice: we are burdened to live with them whether we like it or not. However, accepting their existence and cosigning their reality are two different things. I began making plans to get myself out of that narrow-minded town as quickly as I could. Small-town American life, with its 1950s traditions, may be right for some, but my eyes were on progress.

6 The Lovers

HIGH VIBE · Union, joy, love, attraction, desire, partnership, harmony

LOW VIBE · Discord, incompatibility, loss, disappointment, imbalance

The Lovers represents a decision to move toward a person, place, or thing you value. Whatever's got you turned on and tuned in, the connection can be spiritual, physical, and filled with the promise of enlightenment. There may be a choice at hand as to which direction to move in, or what situation deserves your time and energy. The Lovers are telling you to listen to your heart.

Two vibrant people stand seemingly blessed under heaven's eye, naked before us, in contemplation of union. This card makes people starry-eyed, but it does not always promise romantic love. It's about choices made that move us closer to our dreams.

While The Lovers is all about connection, be it in love or a business partnership, it doesn't always imply the "forever" kind. The future isn't set in stone; bask in your happiness. The important part of this is your connection to spiritual, physical, and self-enlightenment. In other words, the dreamy vibe might not last forever, so enjoy the feelings of the now.

If you pull The Lovers, life may be feeling delicious due to a love interest or intriguing new opportunity, or from having gained a deeper understanding and appreciation of yourself and what turns you on. A giant step toward integration of the different sides of yourself brings a feeling of peace and excitement. You can attract all sorts of interesting characters at this time. Negative internal dialogue is replaced by a deeper connection to intuition and spirit.

In relationship dynamics, a union in the initial blush of attraction, be it love or lust, is felt. Try not projecting too far into the future, as this is not a locked guarantee, but rather a nod to the delicious potential available. For singles, a period of self-actualization is preparing you for love. This is the time to redo your dating profile or ask friends to set you up—Cupid's arrow is pointing at you. Someone unexpected may offer love to you; be open to something different, especially if you've identified patterns keeping you stuck in repeating cycles.

In professional life, a dream job or interview is a sign you're in the right place at the right time. There's an expansive feel in the air; connecting to others and networking can pay off big. If passion is waning, some might decide to switch careers to a field more fulfilling. If this card comes when no prospects are in sight, visualize and journal about your dream scenario, and dust off your résumé.

IF PULLED IN LOW VIBE · To attract love, you first have to love yourself. Emotional and financial burdens, shirking responsibilities, or staying too long in stale, conflict-ridden situations may have caused disconnection and disillusionment. Depression and a lack of desire, drive, or ambition may have created a loss of faith in love or self.

For some, an idealized, unrealistic view of love and interpersonal dynamics creates impractical expectations. Isolation can make it seem as if you're the only one who doesn't have abundance, creating a victim space. Reengage and learn to define and communicate your emotional needs. Love needs a fertile place to grow. If your heart's closed, this card says it's time to open, shift perspective, and make a choice to welcome love into your life.

. . . . . .

It's occurred to me that maybe I should choose a lover, any lover, like immediately, because muscles atrophy and a brand-new final count-down is under way. My DMs are full of retired mailmen from the Midwest who think we'd "be a good match" because they, like me, are old. These men usually lead with a "hey" or "you fine," and I wonder why that is the best introduction they can muster for me, a demigoddess/old-fashioned Victorian lady.

For the past year, my choice has been to focus on work. My tried-and-true life partners are my seventeen-year-old cat and my enfant terrible, a new kitten. Both cats have a patented stare, which I interpret as them psychically willing me to open an extra can of wet food. "Maybe get jobs and contribute to the household, if it's all about wet food" is my stan-dard reply. Talking to my cats usually causes me to check my imaginary watch and say aloud, "Oh my God, I'm in my last five fuckable years."

I want to feel sorry for myself and slip on a coat of victimhood. It would be so easy to hop aboard the pity party train. Alone and covered in pet hair, being eyeballed like a steak by two loud and verbal Siamese cats, I wonder, *When I die, will they eat my eyes?*

Because I am an adult, the way I get out of this headspace is to focus on owning my life choices. Love and the act of being intimate, being truly vulnerable, both sexually and emotionally, is a choice we make when we are brave enough to be present in the company of another person. I have not been that brave very often. In the past, I made an unconscious (maybe conscious) choice to spend most of my time alone, and now the corollary implications of my choices are plain.

One of the many ways I'm working on manifesting a proper lover, a guy I'd consider marrying, is to focus on deconstructing and rebuilding my romantic attachment style. The book *Attached: The New Science of Adult Attachment and How It Can Help You Find—and Keep—Love* by Dr. Amir Levine and Rachel Heller has been helpful in my progress by breaking down the archetypal ways I interact in intimate situations.

I already knew I was an insecure dater. When I dated guys who were hard to get hold of and generally aloof, I spent way too much time thinking it was over if they didn't call me back within six hours. I needed a partner to check in with me on a regular basis, but I didn't feel comfortable asking for this out of fear of appearing clingy.

In this book, Dr. Levine recommends insecure daters ask their partners to do just that: to check in once or twice a day, if they can. The book hit me on the head with the concept of asking for what I need, not imitating what I think sexier, savvier women do around men.

The book also hipped me to my avoidant nature—as in, hiding out on my couch feels safer than actually dating in Los Angeles. It's also my raging ego's way of protecting my soft vulnerable underbelly from being exposed. Women who've strapped on the panoply of armor can sometimes lose the soft, safe place for ourselves and others to land.

I spent the last year examining and setting down old thought patterns and behaviors, like wearing a big bright smile and quick quip as a shield and dating noncommittal guys. I came to understand that this was just a cover for my own intimacy stuff, and was out of alignment with who I'd grown into. I began to appreciate and see the value in my past, finite relationships. Each one of those men taught me valuable lessons; some were loving, some cruel; all highlighted a need to find union and peace within my odd-duck self, and release self-loathing, doubt, and judgment.

Now I'm making the choice to move toward love, and that means becoming comfortable in the company of strangers. Instead of focusing on the ideal perfect mate, I'm working on what kind of partner I'd like to be, so that the next time love comes near, I'll be ready. Tarot, and talk therapy, have been instrumental in my making big leaps in my life. It's a gratifying slog, resulting in an openness to attract the kind of partner I desire, rather than the one I thought I deserved.

7 The Chariot

HIGH VIBE · Victory, will, action, power, success, triumph, opportunity, alignment, balance

LOW VIBE · Failure, force, insecurity, smugness, aggression, brute force, inaction, defeat, missed opportunity

The Chariot signifies success on the worldly plane, an increase in personal power, and a healthy sense of your place in the world. Real-life victories and accomplishments are to be lauded and celebrated, with a reminder: Do not become overly confident or trample those who gave you a leg up.

The Chariot's driver has the serene calm of a victor confident in their win. They bask in a golden yellow glow. Notice the banner hanging above the figure, midnight blue with seven stars, representing a divine alignment (lucky 7s). In one hand they hold a wand; the other is in quiet command of a set of black-and-white sphinxes, representing the opposing forces of our animal nature: physical versus intellectual, masculine versus feminine. There is no gray area in this battle.

Traditionally, sphinxes are riddle keepers. Are they silently celebrating your win, or asking if the victory was worth it? A gracious champion knows good sportsmanship is important, as is a balance between spiritual desires and external material pursuits.

If you pull The Chariot, ambition, effort, decisive action, and exacting plans may have landed you in the driver's seat with a large payoff. This is a card indicating power, control, and self-discipline. The Chariot is the archetypal person who makes it happen now, with decisive action. You are in control and create your own destiny.

In relationship dynamics, forward movement and a new level of commitment may be taking place. The Chariot represents the balance needed to have a successful union, indicated by the previous card, The Lovers (page 73). The Chariot can signify a strong, confident person, one usually used to getting their way. Be careful not to pressure your intended; let things unfold at their own pace. Your partner may need encouragement to break down a tough exterior and unlock a heart they've kept protected. Stand up for yourself if you're being walked on. The key is balancing patience and passion while remaining present. Others may realize it's time to move on and away from a dead-end situation.

In professional life, this is a card of leadership, even if it's a battalion of one. A promotion in status or demonstrative accolades could bring new responsibilities, casting all eyes on you. People will follow your lead and may seek your counsel, especially when you're gracious. If things are rocky, rethink your current endeavors and where your time and energy are allotted. Seize every opportunity and lead, even ones that feel like long shots. Stay diligent and on task; the rewards are worth your efforts. Your ambition, talent, and intelligence are center stage; the universe wants you to shine. Victory is available.

IF PULLED IN LOW VIBE · Perhaps your energy is dragging. Or you've armored up, becoming angry and defensive, always feeling under attack. This can be draining to you and your circle. Remember the old saying: Misery loves company. If this is you, pull it back. Crushing others with control issues or passive-aggressive behavior may need examination. Ill-gotten gains manifest hollow victories.

If you're feeling ground under The Chariot's wheels, or your own ambition has you feeling low vibe, it's time to readjust. Pulling this card can reflect untapped potential, or a missed opportunity you didn't value (or didn't have the patience to see through). A lack of confidence can be crippling. This is a reminder that everything you need to succeed is available; shake yourself out of your rut and back into action. *This is not the time to throw in the towel.* Don't beat yourself up; clarify your plans and charge forward into destiny.

· · · · · ·

I had a couple of things going against me when a friend tossed the script for *The Craft* in my lap.

1: My agent thought I was too old for the part and refused to submit me.
2: I was, in fact, too old for the part.
3: Andy Fleming, the director, had been a super senior at NYU when I was a freshman. We had lived in the same dorm, and *my* roommate had been sleeping with *his* roommate. We'd only met in passing, so I hoped maybe he wouldn't remember me. If he did, pretending to be a high school student wasn't going to work.

Instead of getting down in my feels and stuck in a low-vibration energy, I charged forward. I knew this part was for me. It was everything I'd just devoted study to.

I rang a friend's manager who'd previously asked me about working together. I'd said no, thinking I had agents who covered me and took 10 percent already, so why would I pay someone else another 10 to

15 percent of my earnings? I was about to find out, as I watched my new manager make the phone call my agents hadn't been willing to make. He got me in with exactly one call.

A few days later I strapped on a beaded choker and boarded a tram on the Sony lot in Culver City, heading for the casting office of *The Craft*. It was a quick enough audition; the dialogue wasn't overly complicated. Andy didn't recognize me, thank God. I had a longish monologue to read, where my character, Rochelle, discusses her bulimia, a theme that was cut from the shooting script. I suspect they decided that if Nancy's crisis was her drunk, white trash mother, Bonnie's was her burns, and Sarah's was her suicide attempt, my blackness was a built-in albatross for Rochelle. They later added in the racist swim team character played by Christine Taylor, who's as sweet a girl as you've ever met.

After the audition, I did daily readings with my cards and scooped up every witchy book I could find at the Psychic Eye esoteric book shop in Santa Monica. I placed the printed audition scenes on my altar and visualized myself booking the part, shooting the movie, and having it be popular. I burned dragon's blood, lit candles, called the corners—basically did everything in my power to manifest Rochelle into my life.

Most actors don't like to talk about older roles—it's in the past. I have no problem talking about *The Craft* or my earlier roles because I understand that for a lot of minority women, my roles might've been the first time they saw an odd weirdo black girl portrayed onscreen.

Most black characters I saw in popular movies at the time were not indicative of my personal experience: the 'hood girl who got knocked up at fourteen, the pimp and his hooker with a heart of gold, the first person in her family to go to college, the girl whose drug dealer boyfriend drags her down.

The archetypes are well recognizable, and there were some great and important films that captured this slice of black American life. But Hollywood in no way encompassed the multitude of blackness in America. And in some ways, these roles helped solidify the idea in white American minds that all black people were leading hardscrabble, lower-class lives.

My experience of isolated blackness made it easy to connect with Rochelle. I'd certainly been made fun of in high school for looking different, and I understood the powerlessness of her situation because it was the same as mine. One of the best things about being an actor is getting the chance to relive those moments, only this time with the perfect, professionally scripted comeback.

About a month after the audition (a torturously long time in actor weeks), I was called in to do a screen test. The night before, I did a reading and pulled The Chariot. A good sign. I started going over my crystals and stones, deciding which ones to take with me the following day, when the phone rang. It was Andy Fleming, wishing me luck and giving me encouragement.

"Is there anything I could do to nail the part?" I asked.

"Just don't drool, Rachel, and the part is yours."

I hung up and thought, *Oh God, oh God, oh God, how can I make sure not to drool tomorrow?* I managed about four hours of sleep before I loaded down my jacket pockets with hematite for grounding, rose quartz for calmness, basalt, citrine for creativity and success, and The Chariot card from my Egyptian deck for victory. Excited and ready to meet my destiny, I headed over to Sony feeling my witchy best.

The actual screen test took all day. We had full hair and makeup, and it was lights, camera, action from the word *go*. Robin Tunney, who played Sarah in the film, at that point was reading for the role of Bonnie, which was ultimately played by Neve Campbell.

Fairuza Balk was naturally testing for Nancy and was as intense as you'd think. I'd loved her acting in so many projects . . . I mean, she was *The Worst Witch* growing up and I felt more than a little intimidated and shy around her.

Another actress who was not cast in the film was reading for Sarah, and when we wrapped the test, Fairuza asked her for a ride home, since they were heading in the same direction. She was clearly more freaked than impressed with Fairuza and said no. Robin stepped up and happily gave Fairuza a ride. I often wonder if that "no" cost that actress the lead role.

We'd had a full eight hours of stomping across a sound stage in Catholic schoolgirl uniforms, and I was exhausted, but secretly happy I hadn't seen a roomful of doppelgänger black girls testing for my part.

My agents, who hadn't submitted me for the part in the first place, negotiated a not-great deal for me. The point person handling it told me, "The studio said that's the deal, Rachel, take it or leave it. We have another black girl lined up for the role."

It wasn't true, and I was getting fed up with my agents' whole "You're black, you're lucky to be in any film in the first place" attitude. I accepted the deal, but found new management soon after. The Chariot just keeps moving forward, one battle at a time.

8 Strength

HIGH VIBE · Fortitude, strength, perseverance, willpower, control, courage, lust, sexuality

LOW VIBE · Weakness, indecision, base desire, ego, aggression, confrontation, imbalance

The Strength card represents the struggle between our lower and higher selves; it takes immense strength not to let our low vibes devour us. Inside everyone is the ability to understand, balance, and harness their own vibrational energy.

There is a symbiotic relationship between the lion and the human, and a passivity to the look of this card. The infinity symbol represents the reciprocal relationship between the id and super ego.

If you're being tested, controlled effort and action will bring the desired outcome. Trust that you have the willpower, passion, drive, and determination to grow spiritually as well as materially. Discern when to push forward and when to be still by objectively eyeing your current strengths and weaknesses.

Most of us have a wild side, an inner animal nature intrinsic to our identity. The desires of your ego may propel you forward, but they can also dip you low: seek a balance. The ability to overcome obstacles is available when we have the courage to train and harness the beast within.

For some, exhibiting cool control is advised. For others, breaking free of societal constraints and stepping into your true self is at hand. Kundalini energy, which starts at the base of the spine, or the root chakra (one of the seven chakras, or meridian points of energy, in the body), may be activated at this time, sending the system into sensory overdrive.

In relationship dynamics, some who pull the Strength card may be exploring their true sexual nature and feeling a new sense of freedom. Run with it; move forward, not back. A lusty union of people who challenge and complement one another may be in the stars. Passion and sexual chemistry is high. This comes with the slight danger of overwhelming each other and burning out quickly. Hold your boundaries to manifest the relationship of your dreams.

In professional life, recent developments and accomplishments may have brought more responsibility and attention your way. You are stronger than you think, and equipped for what's coming before you. If difficult tasks are thrown your way, let the boss know you've got the wherewithal to succeed. Some may feel under a gauntlet; the outcome is commensurate to the work put in. Remain levelheaded; a short fuse can get in the way of success. These are the challenges that separate the wheat from the chaff; whoever's left standing is sure to move up the ladder quickly.

IF PULLED IN LOW VIBE · The Strength card is a reminder to stay balanced while fighting for what you believe in. A loop of negative inner self-talk, a lack of direction, or a tendency to lash out in anger may have pulled you off-path. Current feelings of weakness are feelings, not reality; examine how they paralyze or confuse decision making. Understanding your own motivations and emotional triggers makes it easier to temper your reactions and harder for circumstances and people to manipulate you. A habit of giving up when things become difficult and feelings of fear and failure can be shifted. Have courage: this is not a time to give up—it's a time to level up.

·······

A year after my sitcom *Half & Half* went off the air, I got an offer for a film shooting in South Africa. My intuition told me nobody was ever going to see this thing, and truth be told, no one ever did. But the opportunity was impossible to pass up; I love traveling, especially on someone else's dime, and the thought of acting on foreign soil was intriguing.

My first South African shock was seeing brown skin on 90 percent or more of the people I saw on television. We are everywhere: on shows and billboards, hosting news programs, and starring in Harley-Davidson commercials. It was a joy to see.

Half & Half was running on South African network television, and I was getting recognized a lot on the street. On the first day, I went out with the ten or so other American black actresses, and I was fully mobbed, in a way that never happens in the States.

This attention did not engender warm or fuzzy feelings toward me from the ladies. One of the women, it turns out, had tested for the role of my mother, and seemed a little too delighted to spread the information that she and I were around the same age. Typically, actresses don't talk age or money details with random costars they've just met. She broke protocol in an obvious effort to dominate the herd.

I'm proud I didn't give in to my baser instincts, instead saying something sweet and sugary like, "I know, right? Have you always played older your whole career? And you *still* didn't get the part?"

By the time the film wrapped, everybody, including myself, was homesick, but the producers made me an offer to stay longer and travel with a guide to a lion safari in Zimbabwe for some extra filming. I had to do it.

At the enormous no-hunting animal preserve, the lions roam wild and have limited contact with humans once they've grown. "We have a saying here," my guide divulged somberly. "We don't fuck with the lions, and they don't fuck with us."

Several workers were buzzing about having seen my sitcom. I was told I was going to be given a special tour, with close-up access to the lions, while the groups got . . . safety? Look, even minor celebrity has its perks, but usually in the form of free hand creams and decent restaurant tables. But is extra danger really a star benefit?

"The pride took a water buffalo down yesterday; they shouldn't be too hungry," said a tranquilizer-gun-holding park ranger in what I think was meant to be a reassuring tone. I had an epiphany that the word "should" is opaque in its vagueness.

We traveled down a dusty path, sandy reddish soil caking my sneakers. I want to applaud Mother Nature, because I didn't see the first lioness until we were in striking distance from the tree she lounged under. The rangers greeted her and encouraged me to get closer, though I noticed they weren't moving in themselves. "It's okay, you can go. They are wild, but came here when they were young and mostly don't see us as prey. But don't make any sudden movements, okay?"

These are not your average house cats, people. They may purr, lick your hand, and roll around like a kitty, but this lioness was minimum three times the size of the monster Rottweiler that terrorizes my neighborhood. Her liquid gold–gray eyes remained trained on me as I approached. I noticed her ears weren't laid flat back, a sure sign a cat of any size feels uncomfortable. Instead, she seemed curious, and sniffed me as I ever so slowly crouched next to her and looked in the eyes of a badass wild beast. The air felt electric and dangerous, but she looked at me calmly, which in turn calmed my fears.

It occurred to me that this very scene was a literal Strength tarot card moment, and the sort of thing an ancestor of mine might've done many, many moons ago.

The ginormous male was a solid 400-plus pounds of "master of the universe" king lion vibe. I seemed to fall in step with him in relative ease as we crossed the plains. In the end, he was a ladies' man, nuzzling and licking me, which I took as an invite to join his pride. I declined. His fur was softer than I had imagined, his mane a glorious mass of tangles, and his face eclipsed mine to almost Lilliputian stature. My nerves remained on fire, but steady, in a manner I still try to emulate when under stress. To commune with a lion, you must become a lion.

It felt like an out-of-body experience, my own personal version of walking on live coals. I am so grateful for the opportunity to peacefully coexist with these glorious beasts, kings and queens of their domain, beings who hopefully recognized a strong, kindred spirit. By releasing my fear and finding my courage, I was living the vibe of the Strength card.

I know that if I were a mother, I wouldn't let a wild lion lick me with their sandpaper tongue. And there's no way I'd do it again. "Living the Strength card" means knowing when you're being courageous and when you're pushing your luck. The trick is walking the line in between.

9 The Hermit

HIGH VIBE · Introspection, solitude, patience, concealment, wisdom, a spiritual quest, guidance, a mentor, withdrawal, growth, midlife passage

LOW VIBE · Isolation, loneliness, stubbornness, narrow-mindedness, impatience, spiritual crisis, midlife crisis

The Hermit, also known as The Crone, represents The Fool matured.
Now The Fool's journey has a very specific focus: it's a soul-searching quest for wisdom. This card is all about you; not in a selfish fashion, but rather a self-nourishing sojourn.

On this card, a shrouded figure appears to be setting out on, or returning from, a tiresome journey. Which way to go? Which path leads to self-enlightenment, and which leads us down a rabbit hole? It can be a dark dive into our subconscious wild unknown, but The Hermit's lantern provides safe passage as you walk through some deep truths and excise deeper fears.

If you pull the Hermit card, the universe is telling you to take a break from distractions, be they people, places, or things. You've reached a seminal time for personal development. This is not a bad card, per se, but isolation can be a bit sobering, though at times it's necessary for growth. You may not need to be literally alone, but should be cognizant of when you need time for yourself.

People with issues of codependency can receive this card if they're becoming too focused on others. Addicts may also receive this card. It's the dawn of awareness: change needs to happen.

Sometimes The Hermit can represent an enlightened person with information, or someone alone, disinterested in their contemporaries. More often, The Hermit signifies a shifting worldview that changes your perceptions and desires. Coming to terms with your shadow self is possible with the energy of The Hermit.

If you're bummed to see this card, give a think on what feeds your soul. We put off a lot of stuff we'd like to do because nobody else is interested. After some time, we forget the things that turned us on. Reintroduce yourself to you.

In relationship dynamics, The Hermit doesn't always mean a breakup, but you may need to take some time alone or set some new boundaries. This can cause issues in personal relationships if not handled with care. Time spent in reflection will enable you to more effectively communicate your needs. Self-sabotaging behavior can be released, allowing better understanding of your love language.

Some people are tired of being by themselves, and some people feel they don't exist if there isn't someone to witness their being. Depending on where you're at, The Hermit can be an unwelcome card to those wishing to couple, but can give insight into relationship dynamics. This isn't indicative of perpetual singledom, but rather an opportunity to connect with your higher self and become the best you.

In professional life, you may be working solo on a project and have to set your own deadlines or goals. Whether the work is physical or spiritual, this card suggests a deepening process that requires all your attention. Trust that you'll have the drive to see it to fruition. It's important to create space where your vision can grow.

IF PULLED IN LOW VIBE · The Hermit is a reminder to take a journey within, but don't get lost in your own reflection or pulled off-path by glimmering lights in the distance. Overwhelming feelings of isolation, depression, or anxiety can have you lost in a world of your own making. Give a think on what feeds your soul and turns you on. Let your intuition guide you; this is a self-nourishing sojourn, so enjoy the peace and solitude.

······

My initial reaction to the Hermit card, which I personally refer to as The Crone, was peak 1970s Disney: toothless, chin-hair-sprouting, sexless hags, eager to suck the youth out of you. The '70s were a time of unrest, where women's liberation was being discussed. Nonsubservient female archetypes angered the patriarchy.

In my grandmother's day, crones were hormone-imbalancing their way into electric shock treatment. Now these often misdiagnosed independent women are being zapped of their energy by the overprescription of pharmaceuticals. It's not quite as horrifying as being burnt at the stake, but either way, the personal power of independent women is diluted.

I've always been a fiercely independent person. If I ever marry, I could see myself living happily in the house next door to my husband, but I've always dreaded the thought of spending the rest of my life alone. It doesn't help my identity crisis that for most of my career, I played much younger than my chronological years. My age was a closely guarded secret for decades. I was pushing thirty when I played a high schooler in *The Craft*, and I'd started to convince myself that maybe I actually *was* ten-plus years younger. When hanging out with castmates, most of whom were a decade younger, this required a certain amount of creativity in telling my life stories. If someone asked what television shows I watched as a kid, I'd tell them I didn't have a TV growing up.

For a while I was dating a director boy, a nice enough guy, but it just wasn't working out. Two days after I broke up with him, IMDb, which he spent *a lot* of time on, changed my listed age to my real age. *Le sigh*.

BET started blasting my age everywhere. Even I was shocked at the number. Could I really be that old?! Were warts due to grow on my chin at any given moment? I thought about confronting spurned director boy and sending him a bill for all the lost wages I was sure to suffer, but I realized that this was a man who, rather than accept my sexual rejection and move on, had gone out of his way to sabotage my livelihood. Whining to him about it would only give him satisfaction and a sense of power over me.

I did make a call to IMDb to see if I could get my age taken down, to which the guy I got on the phone smugly responded, "We're in the business of facts, so if it's a fact . . ." Obviously I wasn't the first actor or actress to call and voice the same concern.

I considered doctoring up a fake birth certificate like many of my peers had, but I thought of an actress pal who'd lowered her age so far that she rarely booked anything anymore. A director friend who read her recently said, "We wondered if she was ill. She looks so much more . . . tired than you'd think a thirty-five-year-old woman should."

The jig was up. My deep-undercover assignment/torture of moonlighting as someone much younger was at an end. On another level, huzzah, I felt a sense of slight relief to not have to keep so many timeline stories straight.

I decided not to worry about IMDb. Maybe I'd show women that aging is not something to be feared. Occasionally I question the wisdom of this decision, having lived through the dramatic impact it had on my career. After my sitcom ended, I went from playing a character in her thirties to reading for grandmothers overnight.

An actress friend I hadn't heard from for a while rang one day. "Oh, you must feel terrible, it's so awful that your age is out there," she said in a low tone. "I'd die if it were me, everyone talking about my age—you're brave. Gosh, this must be so hard for you, huh?"

I hung up and put this actress friend on my "good to know you're a frenemy" list.

Now I get a fair amount of online attention for looking younger than my chronological age. While it is lovely to have strangers say nice things, it's also bizarre to receive compliments solely for not going full-tilt old-lady crone . . . yet. Plenty of people look young, but I think with me, it's that I'm still incredibly immature and dress like a college sophomore. I'd never really thought about whether I looked young or old, per se. I always attributed it to having a round face and curly hair, but I think it's an energy people respond to.

Now that I'm older and the commodity of youth is no longer at my disposal, my identity and value as a woman have needed to shift. That doesn't crush me as much as it has some of my actress counterparts, but I've never been known as the great beauty. I was the quirky friend. Some of my peers, on the other hand, went nuts. You've seen them: skin too shiny, freshly Juvedermed plump, not looking younger but without a wrinkle in sight, and a worrisome look in their eyes.

Perimenopause and full-on-menopause are a draggy time for some (like me), with very real mood swings and hormone imbalances. Crone energy can be an unwelcome mental burden on top of that; they're a patient teacher one second and a tough bitch the next. But on my way to becoming The Crone, I can't help but push back against the societal image of a sexless old lady, and instead do as the British say: keep calm and focus on the Helen Mirren of it all.

You can be sexy and awesome at any age. The Crone might signify a time alone, but it's almost never a harbinger of your future—more a chance to refocus your energy. Going inward doesn't always mean being alone. I quite enjoy my own company, and find it prepares me best for the company of others.

10 The Wheel of Fortune

HIGH VIBE · Fate, fortune, success, destiny, change, luck, abundance, karma, joyful news, a fresh start

LOW VIBE · Reversal of fortune, bad luck, stagnation, struggle, setback, negativity, lack of control, herd mentality

If you receive The Wheel of Fortune in a reading, it can signify huge shifts and great things coming your way! Jupiter rules The Wheel of Fortune and usually brings rewards.

The tenth card of the Major Arcana, The Wheel is linked to card number 1, The Magician (page 48), and can signify the manifestation of whatever spells The Magician was casting. It also recalls the energy and abundance of the Aces. Major milestones to be celebrated are approaching. If things have been status quo, The Wheel brings a fresh, stimulating new vibe.

For most, this is an auspicious time of good fortune and joy. On the card, the sky is blue, and you can almost feel the sun's warmth. The Wheel is adorned with the signs of the zodiac; how the energy of the stars combine is always a bit of luck, but mostly where you land on the Wheel of Fortune depends on the decisions you make. The Wheel of Fortune represents the cyclical nature of life and, for some, an exciting, happy twist of fate. If you've done some deep digging and a little growing via the lessons of the last card, The Hermit (page 88), the Wheel can bestow gifts for your hard work. Prosperity can come in the form of an unexpected windfall, a chance meeting with a stranger who changes your life, or a small gift, like money found on the street. Stay present, and you're sure to profit during this time of good luck.

Remember, we exist in a constant state of becoming, a "thousand plateaus." The Wheel of Fortune is a reminder that fates can change on a whim. Just as the good times never last, neither do the bad ones.

In relationship dynamics, The Wheel of Fortune can represent people our destinies are intertwined with. A deep soul mate connection may be felt. You may have met or are about to meet a new partner whom it will feel as if you've known forever. Enjoy the exhilaration and remember to take the time to see if your personalities mesh; not all soul mates are life mates.

In professional life, lucrative new ventures may shift your focus in a major way. Be ready for more responsibility and for all eyes to be on you. Behind the scenes, there's information coming that could propel you into high gear. For some, it's time to put in hard work and stop relying solely on luck. You reap what you sow. Act on opportunities; run with the ball when it's thrown to you.

IF PULLED IN LOW VIBE · We're always in motion; sometimes we're up and riding high, other times we're hanging in the middle-ground doldrums, and occasionally every single one of us will experience our version of being ground down to a pulpy dust under The Wheel.

If you're feeling crushed by The Wheel, a less fatalistic attitude and more accountability for your part in why life is the way it is will invite quick positive change. Jealous, petty behavior, envy, and feelings of victimhood or fear of failure/success zap energy and grind The Wheel to a crawl. The Wheel is always turning; start setting up the life you'd like, rather than spinning in anxious negative thoughts or lamenting the fate you were handed. If a sudden enticing offer presents itself, grab it and say yes, even if you're scared. Forces greater than yourself are in play here; use them to your advantage. Setting up an altar and creating vision boards of the life and changes you desire can be forms of meditation and prayer.

. . . . . .

When we were shooting *The Craft*, a young production assistant named Eddie would pick up Neve Campbell and me in his shit-kicked muscle car and take us back and forth to set. We had a blast talking with and teasing him and were surprised when he told us the actors on another production had never engaged him in conversation and were kind of rude to PAs in general. Two years later at Sony, I ran into Eddie, who now had an office on the lot. I thought, *Bet some of those people are wondering why their calls aren't being returned* . . .

I've witnessed power dynamic shifts like this often in my career, and it's an excellent example of The Wheel of Fortune at work. Even when you're on top of The Wheel of Fortune, you still have to keep your balance, because it's an achievement, not a finish line. Things will still be thrown at you. Even when you get the thing you want, like a big role in a movie . . .

After we finished shooting *The Craft*, Neve Campbell called me. "Are you excited for the publicity trip?"

"What trip?"

"Sony set it up. We're going to New York!"

Realizing I hadn't been included, I thought, *I must suck. I'm terrible in the film. Like, how dreadful am I to not be included in an*

Entertainment Tonight *interview?* I felt so very small in that moment. Then I got pissed off.

"This is some bullshit," I said. "I'd be included if I were white." It felt flat-out racist that I hadn't been included. It was a film about four girls, and I'd been told Rochelle had tested high with advance audiences. Perhaps it was simple dollars and cents—they didn't think black people were going to see the film, by and large, so why bring the black chick?

"Well, maybe they left you out because Robin, Fairuza, and I are already famous and you're new." Neve's a lovely girl, who had just turned twenty-one and was starring on *Party of Five* at the time. We'd become fast friends while shooting, but she had told me once that there was no racism in Canada, so I didn't think she was going to get it.

"Uh-huh," I said, and we said goodbye. Ultimately, that's what you do as a person of color in America: you swallow a lot of bullshit.

The next day I got a call from the film's producer, Doug Wick, inviting me to come on the publicity tour. Neve had insisted I be included. I really appreciated her extending herself—not all actors are that generous—but the whole thing left me feeling outside the group.

That night I did a simple reading from my Motherpeace deck and pulled The Wheel of Fortune. I rolled my eyes at first, but then tried to live in acceptance. I thought this film was going to change everything for me, but Hollywood was still Hollywood. I wish I could go back and whisper in my younger self's brain, *This isn't about you specifically; you are simply a sentient being. This is about economics, race, and gender, which are all external things placed onto you by the society you live in.*

I had to talk myself down.

Most people fight against reality. They're mad they're at the bottom of The Wheel. I used it to motivate me. I regrouped, and figured out how to continue to rise. The road to success is rarely as straightforward as A to B—it's more like A, Q, W, F, *then* B. At the apex, at the very top of The Wheel, you better strap in. It's dizzying up in the stratosphere, and much farther of a fall down.

11 Justice

HIGH VIBE · Fairness, honesty, impartiality, fate, karmic law, legal matters, spiritual justice

LOW VIBE · Karmic fate, injustice, dishonesty, lack of morals, gray areas

Pulling the Justice card means the tarot has a message for you: your current situation is a direct effect of choices you've made and how you've been carrying yourself vibrationally through life. Whatever energy you're experiencing correlates to the energy you've previously put out. You get what you give.

The Justice card is a more reactive card than an active/action card. It's a reaction to what is, a reflection of the past. There is nothing you can do about what has already happened except respond to karmic justice. The scales will always balance themselves out in the end. On this card, Justice stands effortlessly on a sword's edge; only by perfectly balancing truth and fairness do they remain unscathed.

If you pull the Justice card, it may signify human justice and the legal system, which is another matter entirely. Some who pull this card may be dealing with a major decision or legal formalities. Be fastidious with the details, and make sure everything's on the up and up. This is not the time for risky or dangerous behavior: assess.

In relationship dynamics, some may be experiencing a deeply felt, balanced connection. Shared respect, love, and appreciation should not be taken for granted. Others may feel unhappy in a current union: acknowledging this can open up a dialogue that creates a better vibe. Consider others when making judgment calls, and treat them as you would like to be treated. It's time to ask yourself how current behavior would be weighed in spiritual court.

In professional life, Justice denotes things moving smoothly and proper credit being given. If you're putting the work in and keeping your energy positive but not seeing the results you want, hang tight. Cause and effect will come into play; continue to be impeccable in your actions and intentions. Trust that things will turn your way, and people who've wronged you and those in low vibration will have to answer when it's their turn.

IF PULLED IN LOW VIBE · While some have a leg up in life, others make their own opportunities. Focus on what is in your capacity to shift within yourself. Not an easy feat when the deck's stacked against you. Fixating on others, past situations, or things out of your control hasn't worked so far. Be clear with your goals, and with where and to whom you give your energy. Take responsibility for your actions to clear past karmic debts.

Examine how you may have contributed to current circumstances; it can be uncomfortable, but taking responsibility is exactly what the Justice card suggests will move you forward most expediently.

. . . . . .

One Friday night I was scrolling through Netflix and was surprised by a picture of me staring back at me. *The Craft* was back on their roster. There I was, pretending to be a petulant teenager. I like the '90s-style optimism on my face and couldn't help but smile back at her.

I promptly unsmiled when I saw that my name, once again, was not listed along with the other three leads in the film's description. It's never *not* annoying.

Maybe they only had room for three names—that's a fair assumption, right? I mean, I was fourth billed in the film. This is a justification I've become familiar with. Because this happens on the regs. I checked a few other films, some of which list more than three actors, and got further annoyed. Was I being Petty LaBelle about it? I tried to stuff my feelings down, as I've been trained as a person of color in America to do. They gurgled back up.

For countless ethnic actors of all flavors, we *accept* and *internalize* these constant oversights, front-slights, and hidden-slights. What other choice do we have? When I began acting, there was a lack of fully-fleshed-out minority roles to be found. Often black actors were relegated to civil servant roles, sassy prostitutes, or, my old standby, the black best friend. I'd been the token in any number of white-centric teen or twentysomething films and shows. Rather than be discouraged or angry, I tried to create the fullest best friend I could. The kind of best friend who left you wondering, *Hey, what happened to that character?* It's decidedly weird to be known as "the black chick in that movie," but it is what it is.

Actor ego aside, being regularly excluded is unfortunate. Representation matters. The sheer amount of cognitive dissonance required to be black in America is utterly exhausting.

Recently, a fan convention invited the three other leads from *The Craft* to appear together. I made it clear I'd also like to be at the convention, but it was made clear back to me that my presence was not wanted.

Fairuza, Neve, Robin, and I had not been in the same room together since 1996. I reminded the convention's director of this fact. An actual reunion would be a big deal; these are the kinds of moments conventions are made for. He did not agree with me, and let me know that even though he'd invited three out of four of us, he "never said we were having a 'reunion.'"

The only thing stopping it from being a reunion was his decision not to invite me; he was leaving money on the table! It was mind-boggling to me until I realized, *Oh yeah, he doesn't think he needs me. He thinks I have no value. He thinks I'm just the black girl from* The Craft.

This would not stand.

I made it clear that I wanted to be added to the convention, or I was going to share my opinions on social media. After twenty-four hours, there was no response from him, so I did.

I didn't think anyone read my posts, let alone that anyone would care. I was wrong: there was an outpouring of attention and support. Fairuza Balk called me to check in, and I told her the situation. "They're gaslighting you," she said. She's always been quick on the uptake, and I appreciated her ability to see the situation outside the prism of herself.

At one point, a representative for a couple of my castmates gave me a statement they'd prepared. I told them I was a grown-ass black lady and comfortable speaking for myself.

Things got ugly all around, and I'm still not sure many of the white people involved in this equation understood my position. After much subterfuge and drama, including an alleged death threat directed at the convention owner, I got an invite, and *The Craft* had our reunion after all.

Having all four us was a lucrative thing for the convention and a highlight for fans. The four of us were absolutely mobbed, with hundreds of people lined up to take group photos. I'm pleased and surprised that many a bearded white man came through my line and made a point to say they loved my Instagram Live "As The Hair Dries Theater" videos and had come specifically to support me.

Speaking out didn't backfire, but it definitely showed me who was who. I still have to remind myself to process and shake off any embarrassment I have over the whole scenario. Since then, I've been humbled by the number of people who've come up to me and told me my actions inspired them to speak up in their own lives, whether it be against a micro- or macroaggression. There was nothing *petty* about having a reaction to being excluded, demeaned, devalued, to being thought of as less because of the color of my skin and kink of my hair. I must remove any unwarranted shame and place the burden back squarely where it belongs: with "The Man," "The System," and, no quotes needed, the inherent racism baked into America that would cloak and drown me if I let it.

12 The Hanged Man

HIGH VIBE · Surrender, acceptance, release,
internal work, acquiescence, sacrifice,
paradigm shifts

LOW VIBE · Struggle, resistance, denial,
submission, myopic vision

The Fool has come a long way on their journey. It's time to pause and reflect.

When you pull The Hanged Man, the tarot wants you to take a beat before proceeding. Don't be pressured or hurried through any decisions; analyze issues from all angles to gain perspective.

The Hanged Man is a pretty straightforward card. There they are, hanging upside down from the tree of knowledge, but they're not tied down. The rays around their head signify the enlightenment that can be found by considering a new perspective. Sometimes you have to put yourself in uncomfortable positions to learn and grow. Surrender to the now, understanding that you do not know everything.

If you're unsure of the best course of action, the best answer may be to do nothing. Let the situation breathe; let the answer come to you. This pause will create a shift in energy, and allow you to view things from a completely new angle. Use this deliberate period of inaction to explore your inner life and prepare for what's to come.

The Hanged Man could represent you or someone close to you who is feeling a bit stuck. Try to look at things with a new set of eyes. Maybe things have slowed down and you feel like you're in a holding pattern. Acceptance of where things are, versus spinning in anxiety over how you wanted things to be, is a crucial step toward forward movement.

Release ego, release expectations, and release outdated attachments; in exchange, you'll get a needed paradigm shift. Energy previously exerted fighting against reality is now freed up to create the desired future.

A spiritual epiphany may be on its way. You may realize that sacrificing short-term pleasures for the greater good of long-term goals resonates with your higher self. For some, The Hanged Man can bring a dawning realization that holding on to what's already gone is the very thing keeping you in stasis.

In relationship dynamics, The Hanged Man does not necessarily imply separation or a breakup, but rather a period of uncertainty or inaction. Roll with it before making any final decisions; this is one of those "only time will tell" scenarios. One partner might want to move things forward, while the other remains unsure. Both parties should sacrifice the need to control the outcome. Some couples may eventually find the inertia too much to bear, while others may realize an inability to release and let go after heartbreak is holding them back.

In professional life, the status quo may continue. Some may find an opportunity to apprentice with a master in their field, while others learn the hard way that forcing someone's hand and trying to control a situation will not help them achieve the desired outcome. Take this time to rest and regenerate; see what's been gleaned, gained, or lost since your last self-check-in.

IF PULLED IN LOW VIBE · Stillness speaks its own language, but staying in stasis too long means you're stuck. Fear of failure or success may have you feeling indecisive, isolated, and/or depressed. Get out of your head and reconnect with the rituals, people, and places that give you comfort. Ask yourself what you're putting off, what's stealing your joy, and what is within your power to shift. Surrender old negative behavior patterns and tune into your inner voice for guidance.

······

At twenty-three, I was living in an apartment in New York's East Village directly across the street from a building I had lived in as a small child. I had two random NYU undergrad bros for roomies, was doing commercial work, and was generally living a very Tama Janowitz/*Slaves of New York* kind of gal-in-the-big-city existence.

My love life, meanwhile, hadn't so much stalled out as never really begun. My only relationship of any notable length had been with "The Gay College Boyfriend," which at the time left me woefully unprepared for how to interact with a man *not* living a double life.

I wasn't focused on romance when I met a dark-haired, cleft-chinned, chocolate-eyed, "what in the name of the gods is this soul connection from another timeline" kinda vibe man. I was schoolgirl smitten, and he was equally infatuated and bewitched by my charms.

He was a grad school TA, a few years older, transplanted from England, raised partly in France. He'd gone to Eton and had the posh accent to match. Half-Jewish, half-Italian, and completely mesmerizing to an American girl raised on the empty promises and fumbled passes of typical frat boys.

The next time we saw each other, we grabbed Indian food, of which neither of us ate very much, then went back to my place and didn't leave my bed for three days. This was not at all my style; I longed to be courted and wooed. It was worth the break in tradition; I was, it turns out, a novice when it came to actually making love and/or being sexually exploratory. He was the archetypal King of Wands, delighted to indulge in something he clearly considered a fine art.

I nicknamed him the Nomad Poet due to his extensive travel and his habit of writing me a poem every day. For the next few months, we made love, shot black-and-white short films with his Super 8 camera, and smoked a metric ton of Marlboro cigarettes and weed. Whenever I asked my cards about him, The Lovers, The Devil, and The Hanged Man would show up, which always had me, well, hung up. The Hanged Man brought a message of stasis and inertia, but what else? What does "surrendering to the now" really mean?

In springtime, New York City comes to life in a way that rivals Paris, but spring also signaled my guy's inevitable departure back to London for the summer, possibly forever. One rainy May night, after handing over a thatch of love poems he'd written, Nomad Poet asked my relationship expectations.

My desire for matrimony and monogamy popped to mind, but didn't ring true in this situation. I was completely in love, but also an occasionally practical girl. Our glaring difference was always status and class, pomp and formality (not the construct of race or a gap in intellectual compatibility). But our biggest problem was that his Lothario ways wouldn't work for me long-term. Neither of us was ready to set down roots, and I knew he'd rarely resist sleeping with any woman he found intellectually intriguing. I never considered dating someone there was no future with, but it felt right in this circumstance. I finally realized why The Hanged Man kept showing up in my spreads.

"Listen," I said, "I'm not looking to get married. I'm super focused on getting my career off the ground, and whatever this is, it probably won't last forever. Let's just enjoy each other right now."

We spent as much time together as we could in that vein, until the dreaded day he was off to Europe. He sent me daily packages of love poems. Within a few weeks, he sent me a ticket, along with a plea to join him. My friends and family told me not to go; I sent them all postcards from Paris, with a thoroughly pretentious quote: "Nothing had been shattered, except my illusions."

These were heady times, and they continued for a couple of years. I discovered my love of French film noir, Italian cooking, more sex, more weed, and the more than occasional psychotropic. We traveled London, Paris, the Netherlands, and Jamaica, where he used his brand-new Nikes as collateral to bribe our way out of being carted off in a paddy wagon for weed possession. We drank so much coffee at Cafe Mogador in the East Village that if you squint, you'll see our specters poring over poetry books. I delighted when the Nomad Poet introduced me to the philosophy of Pierre-Félix Guattari and Gilles Deleuze, and the aphorisms of Antonin Artaud, though I told him I needed a break when we got to Martin Heidegger. We were a good fit; my vibe could mellow, de-stuff, and expand him, while his poetry, keen artistic mind, and intense sexuality awoke me.

Along with the artistic freedom that came with our relationship, there was plenty of upheaval, heartbreak, and tears. Which is my future-jump way of saying, the stormy breakup inevitably came. There was distance and time between us for a while, until, like elastic, we snapped back toward our center. Now as adults, we are extremely close, and cultivate a fully platonic if flirty friendship with healthy boundaries, respect, and admiration for one another. We remind each other of a very specific period in our lives, and we encapsulate each other's youths.

Even though he wasn't my forever soul mate, he was absolutely a soul mate. The life experience and growth we shared shaped us both into the people we are today. Perhaps I was in stasis during my time with him, but what I learned during that time was invaluable.

13 Death

HIGH VIBE · **Rebirth, release, opportunity, second chances, change, endings, transformation**

LOW VIBE · **Change, fear, obsession, abandonment, denial, stagnation**

The Death card represents a clearing away of the people, places, things, and ideologies that no longer serve you. Release that which is out of alignment and transform.

Generally the most feared card of the tarot, it's really just misunderstood. The Death card represents more a death of ego, or a death of your old self, than an actual death. Rebirth and transformation are the main themes here. Changes currently under way will ultimately remove obstacles in the path of your personal growth. Death claws away at its own decay, revealing new life underneath. This transformation is an eternal process.

For some, the Death card brings a welcome relief; there's a well-lit path away from past sadness and losses. Clarity is here. This may require actively deciding to move out of denial and mourning. For some, a period of anxious mental exhaustion is coming to an end.

If you feel stuck, the Death card signals a new life is quite close. This can be a heavy or fearful period for some, or one of lightness for others, depending on the prism through which you view change. It might be time for a paradigm shift around expectations and attachments, of yourself and others.

In relationship dynamics, some may see a past love return in high vibe. Others know releasing stagnant energy makes room for new love. This can feel tender and delicate. It's possible to nurture a deeper physical and psychic connection to your partner or yourself currently. Some who pull the Death card in high vibe may feel ready to open their hearts again after grieving a loss.

In professional life, a lucrative prospect may have gone away or, alternatively, resurfaced after a period of inaction. Explore all options and don't bet all your money on one horse; there may be changes coming you're unaware of. Some may be leaving current jobs to follow a whole new career path. Hubris and ego need to be watched in order to ensure a successful outcome. Choose your battles wisely; focus on what's still in play.

IF PULLED IN LOW VIBE · Every ending brings a new beginning. Clinging to what has already passed away may be keeping you trapped in a cycle of depression, anxiety, and fear. Obsessively replaying rejections keeps the vibe low. Great things come to those willing to walk through the discomfort of transformative change. Moving away from an old life into something brand-new can be scary, but it's exactly what's needed. Trust that whatever's moving out and on will clear the way for an ideal situation or relationship. Your personal power is not lost. It's time to rise from the ashes, like the phoenix you are, into your new life.

......

The Death card represents transformation of self, a concept Scorpios like myself are fantastically familiar with. Scorpios are the natural detectives of the astrology world, and symbolize transformation. Ruled by the planet Pluto, which is named after the Roman god of the underworld, the Death card is a perfect fit. Life is constant motion, whirling in a perpetual state of transmutation. Even in true and final death, the physical state transforms into bone meal for the worms and fertilizer for the crops. I'm reminded of the Japanese philosophy of wabi-sabi: nothing is perfect, nothing is complete, and nothing is permanent.

Ego deaths and their subsequent aftermaths are life's stock in trade. I can vividly recall the ego deaths of my childhood: waiting on a curb for a parent who doesn't show, or for calls that never came. These felt like full-stop rejections to my young, self-focused brain. It's assuredly an ego death that transforms us into autonomous, if not quite trusting, adults.

When I found out I'd booked *The Craft*, a studio film, which in actor-speak is the equivalent to winning the Powerball, I felt an elated rush of serotonin, but also, tucked up in the nooks of my brain and crannies of my body, I detected a thread of fear. *Was it just a fluke that I was so good in the audition room? What if I suck, and they fire me and I don't get to be a movie witch? What if my tongue stops working? What if my eye twitch comes back? What if I can't lose ten pounds before shooting*, etc., etc.

I felt like a fraud, and that I didn't deserve good things, even though I had earned my part, same as everyone else. That's called impostor syndrome. It was time to look impostor syndrome in the eye and tell it, "It's not you, it's me . . . we're breaking up." I needed to stop apologizing for not being quite as "talented, beautiful, or fabulous" as the person sitting next to me.

As we began the rehearsal process for *The Craft*, one of the other actors snapped at the director, "Is she going to say it like that?" in reference to a line I'd just delivered. This was embarrassing, but I had to admit, the line had tripped and thudded, landing under my tongue rather than slipping gracefully off it. Instead of fully sinking into mortification or defending my reading, I said, "No. I'll say it like this," and the right reading materialized.

Transforming into someone who didn't crumple at criticism, especially the kind coming from fellow actors, an on-set no-no, meant killing off the part in me that wanted to take offense. Transforming this energy into a more positive willingness to attempt and fail is what a creative life is all about.

During the actual shoot, I picked up a lot by listening and paying attention. When the director of photography cupped my face in his hand, moved it from side to side, and finally pointed to the left side of my face and stated, "This is your better angle," I listened. Rather than lament or self-obsess about not being perfect, I acknowledged that my face was far from symmetrical and that my jawline was stronger on the left. I began to subtly favor that side until this action became automatic. A simple move took me from cute to pretty on a thirty-foot-tall screen and went permanently into my actor's bag of tricks.

Every time a job ends or begins, an actor suffers the slings and arrows of any number of deaths. We did most of the green-screen work for The Craft in the last few weeks of shooting. It was more tedious than creative, and after months of shooting, I was ready to wrap up. Luckily, I went right into shooting Gregg Araki's Nowhere. Finally, I understood why people jumped from relationship to relationship without a gap; there's no time to process and mourn the death of what was when you're already on to what is or what would be.

Transforming, for me, has usually meant relinquishing the constrictive amniotic blanket of who I thought I was to bloom into who I'm meant to be. I am nothing if not constantly rising from the metaphorical ashes, albeit at times from fires of my own making. The very nature of being alive means having to process difficulties without letting it debilitate life or derail dreams. Actors know the show must go on, and every Death card pulled signifies a brand-new, Fool-card beginning.

14 Temperance

HIGH VIBE · **Equilibrium, synergy, healing, creation, moderation, forgiveness, maturity, harmony, recovery**

LOW VIBE · **Imbalance, stagnation, confusion, disconnection, addiction, lack of focus, lack of boundaries**

The Temperance card is a sign you're experiencing spiritual clarity and/or mental maturity. You're realizing that knowledge and peace sought externally reside within.

An angelic figure stands with one foot in the water, one on land: a balance between intuitive emotional nature and concrete reality. They're pouring cups into one another, signifying synthesizing two sides of the self. This mixture of two things is alchemical and creates something new. The circle around the figure's head represents the opening of the third eye. Mountains in the background signify there is more enlightenment to be attained.

The Temperance card represents a shift into connection with your higher self and true purpose. If recent transitions have thrown you off balance, the tarot is asking you to grow in a more graceful fashion. Be gentle in how you speak to yourself while sticking to new plans. Art therapy and other creative endeavors can help soothe the soul.

Temperance may represent a teacher, spirit guide, guardian angel, or your own inner Magician giving a big thumbs-up or a knock on the head. Some may still be mourning past losses; use this time to connect to your intuition. Revelations about past misconceptions are possible; you may feel connections to others in profound new ways.

Sometimes, Temperance comes up in readings for people entering treatment for addiction. Maybe you have lost your ability to balance your consumption of food, drink, or drugs. Take heed of the Serenity Prayer: "God, grant me the serenity to accept the things I cannot change, the courage to change the things I can, and the wisdom to know the difference."

In relationship dynamics, Temperance indicates you've made it past the puppy love of the Lovers card. A desire to connect on a deeper spiritual level is felt. Some couples may feel on more equal footing after a period of disparity. Some are contemplating marriage. If things have been moving a little too quickly, Temperance may be telling you to cool off a bit. Singles may be opening their hearts and minds to an inspiring new person. One partner or both may be considering giving up a vice or shared activity. Lead with compassion as your loved one grows into their true self.

In professional life, you may be feeling up to any tasks thrown your way. A thoughtful approach makes you an integral part of team success.

New hires at work may have insightful information to contribute; help them acclimate, and they'll champion you. Others may be considering going into a new business partnership or following a new path altogether. Temperance is telling you to go for it in a calm, cool, and collected manner.

IF PULLED IN LOW VIBE · Temperance can indicate a need for moderation. Address imbalances, especially in how you handle physical/emotional pain. For some of us, that means possibly letting go of habits, and for others, finding the right balance.

It's important to note that anxiety can be addicting, and a lot of Americans are stuck in a spiral of negative thought patterns, purposely engaging in activities that stop forward motion and letting depression, anxiety, and overwhelming fear take over. Stay grounded, balanced, and connected to your higher self.

. . . . . .

In the '90's I played Mary Jane, Dave Chappelle's love interest in the stoner film *Half Baked*. Being Mary Jane has its perks; even though in the film I played something of a teetotaler, in real life, I can go anywhere in the world and be offered a joint.

There was no actual pot smoking on set; all the weed in the film was fake. It would've been incredibly unprofessional to roll in bleary-eyed, forgetting lines, or coming off unfocused because we couldn't wait a few hours to get high. What the *Half Baked* cast was up to after hours is another story that involves many laughs, joints, and an occasional hallucinogenic.

For me, marijuana has a desirable quality and helps with my anxiety. Some smokers have more of an addictive reaction to pot, but I've been able to cultivate a balanced usage, for the most part. That's what the Temperance card is all about: balance.

In high school, I had almost zero experience with or interest in drugs. Taking a handful of mail-order speed a schoolmate bought from an ad in the back of a heavy metal magazine quelled any thirst. It felt like I was being hit in the head with a wooden mallet, and I could feel my heartbeat thudding all the way down into my toes. I was convinced I was going to die. Speed's just not my thing.

On a junior year hangout, someone stuffed a tab of acid in my mouth, which I promptly spit out when they weren't looking. I pretended to see the same trippy colors and shooting stars everyone else was experiencing. Hallucinogenics weren't the norm, although once I did a hit of acid and went to the Bronx Zoo, where I saw no animals, nary a one.

My dad smoked pot regularly to stem his anxiety and abate his then undiagnosed bipolar symptoms. He'd get stoned and talk for hours about time travel, medieval art, or the pitfalls of his generation's ethos. The twists his mind made fascinated me; he was a clever man, bordering on brilliant. But he did tend to drag on. I thought weed made people self-indulgent, at least on the storytelling front.

My older brother smoked pot he'd nick off my dad's stash. We weren't the closest siblings, but I kind of get why he might've felt a need to escape mentally; he was the only black male in a fifty-mile radius. Kids have a voracious need to escape from the world they've inherited. Drugs offer that, with a price.

In college I roomed with a photographer/very minor weed dealer and lost an entire winter to Chocolate Thai stick, a strain of marijuana that bolts you to the couch, forces you to eat anything in sight, and zaps your motivation.

That same winter, Ecstasy was hitting the scene, and my then boyfriend and I did five hits in one week, which I really do not advise. While interesting from a therapeutic standpoint, X makes a weird casual drug, in my opinion: a chemical caul that makes you love everyone you see, but zaps your serotonin levels, leaving you depressed and out of sorts for far too long afterward.

The most worrying aspect of this hazy high winter was that while I was making a decent living bartending, a job I could do high as a kite, I hadn't made any forward movement toward being an actor. Supporting myself solely off my art was always my goal.

I went for a walk early one morning, and the sky and trees looked so clear and crisp that it hit me that it was the first time in months I'd gone anywhere not baked. I probably hadn't even seen a movie sober since freshman year.

It was clear I'd overdone it. I was supersaturated, out of balance, and it was time to dry out. Being an actor was more important. Luckily for me, I found pot to be more a habit than an addiction. It took a few weeks to break that habit, but feeling better and being more creative was worth it.

Eventually I went back to smoking marijuana. I found a strain I call "bionic weed" that shuts down my anxiety and keeps me creative. I find marijuana in moderation useful for its medicinal benefits, whether it's in CBD or THC. There are many studies to back this up. We have cannabinoid receptors for a reason. I also appreciate it as a tool to shift perceptions and dip us into the unconscious. I find it useful during the development stage of learning a role. I'd never smoke on set, though; you need to be fully present to act. Some personality types cannot find balance with any sort of enhancement, plant or chemical. It is important for people who get the Temperance card to be realistic.

15 The Devil

HIGH VIBE · **Release, awareness, liberation, choice, sexuality**

LOW VIBE · **Ego, addiction, lust, codependency, temptation, illusion, weakness, debauchery, delusion, materialism**

The Devil signifies our internal struggles with external temptations, and the choices we have in the matter.

A goat-faced man appears on a bright blue day. He lords over a dark space, filled with the earthly remains of humanity, symbolizing a loss of spiritual connection.

In the foreground kneel The Lovers, a direct link to the sixth card of the tarot (page 73). Where once they had true love, now the innocence of their union is lost. They left the garden, indulged in some vices, and picked up a few new habits. Chains bond the pair together, keeping them codependent and attached to their addictions. They must examine what's working and what's lowering their vibe before they're kicked out of paradise, again.

Facing things we've chained ourselves to, some of which are dragging us down, is never easy, but is strongly advised. If you pull the Devil card, take it as a sign: you're playing with fire.

Instead of getting Judeo-Christian uptight and freaked out about this card's imagery and name, in its high vibe, the Devil card's energy is more like Pan, the sexy drunken party god. An internal awakening and/or pull toward societal taboos, sexual or otherwise, means an intoxicating, debauched devil of a good time can be had, but only as long as no one gets hurt.

At its gentlest (and let's face it—it's a pretty rough card), The Devil represents a need to remove your rose-tinted shades and examine patterns of destructive behavior and questionable motivations. The Devil is a sign that your lower-vibration self, the shadow self, is more in control than has proven useful. There's no use trying to banish the lower self, but you want it less in control, or at least I do. The chains that bind you to bad behaviors, and your bondage to negative thinking, can be undone only by acknowledging your own complicity.

The vibe of the people surrounding you is important, and the Devil card may be telling you to let go of frenemies who don't have your best interests at heart, as well as any toxic dynamics. Perhaps you're involved with a partner who isn't good for you, or you're taking too many drugs, binge eating, or stuck in a victim mentality. If you're feeling trapped in a dead-end situation, the Devil card says break the chains. Notice that the shackles binding The Lovers on this card are not so tight that either party couldn't shrug them off and walk away. It's okay to ask for outside help if your life feels out of control.

In relationship dynamics, you may be feeling a sexual liberation, or a strong pull toward a sexy, charismatic new person may have you in a fever state. Check in if you've been distracting yourself rather than dealing with painful emotions. Communicate needs truthfully and get all the details out before committing your heart. If you're ignoring any bad vibes they're giving off, The Devil can be a sign to look closer. Some liaisons enlighten, and some leave us teetering on the abyss of a spiritual void. For some, addressing issues of codependency, sexual dysfunction, or repression will lift dynamics to a healthy place. Others need to make sure they are on the same emotional page as their partner; someone may have stronger attachments.

In professional life, The Devil can indicate things may not be what they seem. Offers that sound too good to be true probably are. Subterfuge can be afoot, so keep your eyes open—some people may be wolves in sheep's clothing.

The temptation to take shortcuts or credit for others' efforts indicates low self-worth and a need to refocus and appreciate your own talents and gifts. The choices you make define your personal morals and code of ethics. Ask if your ambitions and actions are in alignment with your higher self.

IF PULLED IN LOW VIBE · Be aware of the seven deadly sins when the Devil card is pulled: pride, greed, lust, envy, gluttony, wrath, and sloth. Do you recognize yourself carrying this energy? Everything we're attracted to may not be good for us. If you're aware of your own negative behavior and choose to continue, know you may attract situations that put you in dicey spots, emotional or otherwise. Your daily habits and associations may be holding you back from moving into the life you want. Depression, anxiety, and fear can leave you vulnerable and paralyzed, in a victim space, blaming others. Mentally numbing out the mind can lead you to unsavory interactions. Let go of the pacifiers anchoring you to old paradigms and put your higher self first.

. . . . . .

Not long after I moved to LA, I fell head over heels in love with a beautifully stunning man who had gold dust in his shoes and big fame in his future.

The Actor, a man/boy with perfect '90s hair, had a brilliant million-watt smile that shone to the sun and back. It was love at first sight for both of us, by both accounts. Weird and silly, here was a goofball to match my own out-of-step rhythm. It seemed destined to be the greatest love of all . . . until it wasn't.

He was the epicenter of his social group, with everything on his terms; I've found this often to be the way with those near to stardom. We were cast together in a TV movie, and he didn't seem thrilled, which should have been a red flag. He ignored me the whole shoot, instead flirting with the costumer, who laughed when I mentioned that we'd been dating for months.

My personality disappeared around him. I was fearful I'd say something that would send him into the arms of the many B-level actresses lounging in the wings and in his bedroom on the nights he didn't see me. I wanted him to love me as desperately as I loved him. I got smaller and lower in vibe and energy as he became more distant.

Despite the distance, despite it all, there was intense passion and magic in our connection. When it ended due to his cheating, he offered his friendship in earnest, but I was broken, consumed with myself and spinning in an ocean of emotional pain, the depth of which I'd never encountered before. Worst of all, my underlying raging abandonment issues had been triggered.

A few months later, I accidentally-on-purpose ran into him at a Valentine's Day house party. His crowd was with him, and memories of past snickers had me spinning. I was head-over-ego in my feels, in a panicky state, and blaming the Actor for everything, with no ownership of my part. It hadn't occurred to me to ask myself why I'd ever stayed in a situation where my needs weren't being met.

At one point I found myself alone outside with him. As he talked, I dwelt on how every person at the party knew he'd cheated on me, serially. He was mid-story, offering up a not-remotely-humble brag about fooling people into thinking he was a member of the rock band REM and then being rewarded for his lie with VIP treatment, including a hotel hookup in Vegas. *He's just as much a liar as ever*, I remember thinking bitterly.

He was saying something like, "So then we were given a suite at the Hard Rock . . ." when everything went white and hazy and I just socked him. For the first, and thankfully last, time in my adult life, I hit a human in anger. It's a horrible, terrible, no-good thing to have done, and it's something I will always regret. How I handled my emotions in this situation was unacceptable and frightening to me as well as to him. Though clearly I wanted him to feel some of the pain he'd caused me, this was not my lesson to teach, and certainly not in that manner.

It was an eruption that eventually brought to light for me how I mimicked my father's behavior and used a shield of anger to not feel emotions and to distance myself from people. Even more necessary to understand, I was chained to a pattern of thought that was no longer serving me well. My father problem-solved by having tantrums and breaking things he loved, including people. And like my father, I'd hurt a person I had once loved very much. My pain had brought out The Devil in me.

That night, I couldn't stop thinking about my upbringing. Growing up in an environment where I had to vie for attention had made love feel conditional, so I'd always assumed that when a man fell out of infatuation with me, the mission was to convince him to change his mind, to reignite that attention. I'd taken the slights and the subtle disinterest as challenges, rather than the passive-aggressive signs that it was time to move on. I'd always assumed a guy would just end things with me cleanly rather than torture me into doing it for him. The terrible way I handled this breakup forced tremendous epiphanies.

I asked a happily married friend of mine to lunch one day, hoping to find out her secret. She had had several successful relationships with men who adored her before she settled down.

"It's incredibly simple, really," she said. "I only date men who are a hundred percent into me."

"How do you know they're all the way into you?" I said.

"I dated a guy once who was amazing the first few weeks, but then he started only making last-second plans. We'd be out to dinner, and he'd flirt with other girls right in front of me."

"I would've smacked him," I said.

"Yes, all of Hollywood knows you would've smacked him."

I threw a breadstick at her.

"At first I thought he was making me feel small and low, but then I realized it was me; it was my choice to be with him. I vowed never to put myself in that position again, and broke up with him easily."

Not long after the end of our relationship, a pal told me a friend of hers had gone on a date with the Actor and was turned off because there were "too many drawings of a black girl called Rachel" around his apartment. Muse energy, I'll take.

A year or so later, I ran into the Actor at a film premiere and immediately apologized for my trespasses. He was slightly tipsy, friendly, and as charming as ever. He told me he had really loved me and was sorry for how he had treated me. Just then, Winona Ryder walked over and told me I was pretty. It felt like closure, and at that moment, all was right with the world.

16 The Tower

HIGH VIBE · **Abrupt change, release, spiritual epiphany, transformation**

LOW VIBE · **Conflict, setback, anger, revelations, chaos, endings, unstable foundation, decimation**

The Tower represents a dramatic release of tension, a shattering of illusions, and a breakdown of the status quo, leading to deep transformation.

This can happen on the physical plane, as suggested by the card's imagery, or through self-realization, leading to spiritual enlightenment. The transition can be rocky.

On the Tower card, we see a seemingly impervious dwelling being torn asunder by lightning, signifying a jolt to consciousness, a falling away of the status quo, old ideas, and behavior patterns. In a sense, this card represents death, or an ending, even more so than the actual Death card (page 107).

The Tower's impact need not always be negative, but rather a nod that something unexpected, big or small, may be on the way. The lightning bolt can hit with an uplifting revelation or tremendous destruction; the lesson, ultimately, is how well you handle emotional and spiritual upheavals. This can feel like a "hard lesson now, gratitude later" moment in your life. Those resistant to change or harboring control issues may find this a challenging time.

In Judeo-Christian beliefs, there is a story of the Tower of Babel. Man, who spoke a common tongue in biblical times, built a tower to reach the heavens, so they might drop in on God whenever they wanted. Hubris personified. God was like, *Yeah, no thanks*, and *For bothering me, I'm going to give you guys many different languages so you are unable to communicate with each other*. Thus the term "babble." This story is a parable, a warning against going after something you think you really want without considering the ramifications.

The Tower is the ultimate wake-up call. Anything built on a false foundation is exposed and destroyed. Dead-end situations are swept away. Sudden change feels like sandpaper on the skin, but it usually dumps us out somewhere much better.

This card is in part about blowing up ego (the parts no longer serving us) by not flinching from our lower shadow self (revealed by the Devil card) and the reflection given. Sometimes you have to stare into the abyss of self without blinking, and trust that what is being cleaved away is for your betterment.

This is one of those heavy cards; there's no way to sugarcoat it. It's like when the hero in a movie thinks everything's going to work out, but then an unchecked detail or backstab blows up the plan. In script writing, it's called "the high tower surprise." The aftermath of this is "the dark night of the soul."

In relationship dynamics, expect the unexpected. Emotions and tempers can flare when things feel unstable. Be truthful, lead with compassion, and check your impulse to act out of emotion. Get to the root issues bringing down romantic dynamics. Some may find that a sudden ending creates a rocky landscape at home, while others get an unexpected addition to the family.

In professional life, a select few could receive a sudden promotion and change in title. Most others will see things shift rapidly; stay on top of the details and on your toes. You can't control circumstances or others at this time, and exerting might will prove frustrating. Sometimes The Tower can signify an internal explosion of anxiety and stress. Be careful of reactive behavior; if it is within your personal power to shift this energy, do so.

IF PULLED IN LOW VIBE · When you don't clear out what's not working, the universe has a way of doing it for you. Misdirected anger, volcanic tempers, overreactions, and/or blaming others is a sign of spiritual turmoil, which keeps you in a state of disconnection, feeling isolated and alone.

If you don't have the power to control a shifting situation, you can only control your response to the new landscape. If you understand this, you can soften, misdirect, and blunt the blow of The Tower. Current challenges are here to make you grow and put you back on the right path. The Tower sweeps away negative patterns and habits revealed by the previous card, The Devil. It's time to transform your life.

. . . . . .

My younger brother, Roc, and I didn't grow up together. The first time I met him, he was four years old and reminded me of the kid in the original *Mad Max* movie. As an adult, he lived in Pismo Beach, and one year he came down to LA with his fiancée and attended a taping of *Half & Half*. He was super excited and encouraging. Everyone could tell he was my brother; he looked just like me.

I went to Roc's wedding soon after, with a guy everyone called Powder, because he was translucent in look and thought. Powder had an intense Peter Pan complex and fronted a celebrity vanity band. I remember watching Roc, the archetypal surfer dude, marry the woman of his dreams, and I started thinking about children and settling down. Roc and his bride had been together since they were teenagers and had never once had an argument, he'd said. And there I was, in a relationship that was my personal nadir. I wasn't in love with Powder, and feared he'd father a beautiful but dense child, and that wouldn't do.

The wedding went smoothly, for the most part. I hadn't seen my birth mom in almost a decade. She offered Powder and me each a handful of white pills from a plastic bag in her purse, while her husband, Roc's father, bored us with stories of his musician glory days. "This one time when we played the Roxy . . ." It hit me that Powder was a carbon copy of him, down to his scraggly, aging-hair-band appearance. How mortifying. What was I doing with my life, besides repeating the patterns I'd experienced growing up?

When the party was over, I kissed my brother goodbye and promised to try to be closer to our mother.

For months after the wedding, I felt an intense sense of dread. I chalked it up to changing hormones and assumed it was a medical thing, but I couldn't shake the feeling, like I was waiting for a giant cowboy boot to come out of the sky and smash me.

One gloomy day in Los Angeles, I looked up, trying to decide if it was going to start raining, and saw a small bird attacking a sitting squirrel it had apparently taken umbrage with. The squirrel tried to escape, scrambling the length of my wooden fence, the perniciously aggressive bird far getting the better of it. *Oh no*, I thought. *Something's just gone out of whack.*

My cousin called to tell me. Roc was dead at twenty-eight. He'd had an epileptic seizure.

It was hard to accept that a twentysomething person could be gone. The whole thing was so shocking, I had a delayed reaction. He did have a history of seizures; when we were kids, he'd lose chunks of time. Our mother thought he'd been abducted by aliens.

While I know Roc is gone, I quite often still feel his energy around me. And I can imagine the shock and utter joy several families in America experienced when they received a call that the heart, lungs, kidneys, and corneas of an up-until-yesterday healthy young male were available for their relative in need. As utterly shocking and devastating as this was for my family, the high vibe of The Tower was influencing those families as well.

I could write pages on how horrible it is to lose a loved one who had so much ahead of him. But the truth is, most of you have experienced what I'm talking about. I'll leave it at that.

17 The Star

HIGH VIBE · Healing, optimism, hope,
inspiration, liberation, replenishment,
compassion, release, renewal, faith

LOW VIBE · Oppression, depression,
stagnation, despair, hopelessness, illness

The Star represents a release from burdens, and lights up the pathway to your desired future. Hope has arrived.

A lot of people who pull The Star smile quickly, because "The Star" connotes a happy card, and yes, it is a *great* sign that things are going to get way better. This card is the calm after the storm. It's about keeping faith more than a current cause for celebration.

A solitary figure is presented, naked, stripped of their previous identity, released from judgment. One of their feet is on water: emotional calmness and equilibrium. The other is earthbound: mental and physical grounding. Together, they're taking thoughts and manifesting them into reality. Each hand releases a cup, one on land for the physical self, and the other into the collective unconsciousness.

The eight stars above connect to the body's chakras, and The Star is directly connected to the eighth card of the tarot, Strength (page 83). The Star has more of a chill vibe. You may be surprised at your own inner strength and feel relieved, serene, accepting, and grateful for a new vibe. You may be feeling emotionally lighter. This is the moment when things begin to tip in your favor, so plan accordingly.

Most of the changes and upheavals you've recently undergone are beneficial in the long term, but short-term, they sure can burn. Here is where the cooling waters of The Star come in handy. This card often represents someone who has emerged from the shackles of victimhood to heal their inner wounds, setting themselves up for future success.

Some are already experiencing illumination and riding a wave of forward momentum. You may find you're able to remain calm and centered despite external calamity. You may be releasing a creative project, or offering up your work to the world. It is yours, but you can't control how people think about it. You must simply release it.

There are similarities to Temperance, the fourteenth card (page 111). Temperance is more about synthesizing sides of the self; The Star is about release. This is often the card that comes up after a breakup, on that first day when you wake up knowing that you're ready to move on. It's a good feeling, but that doesn't necessarily mean you're smiling.

In relationship dynamics, you may feel an affinity or pull toward an alluringly calm, cool, and collected person who recently entered your stratosphere. For couples, there's a feeling of centered connectedness. Others may go through a cooling-off period; roll with it, and you may gain deeper understanding. For those unhappily attached, The Star is a gentle reminder that rather than expend energy pushing for reconciliation, you should focus on healing and raising your own vibration.

In professional life, some find themselves at the top of their field after a tough climb. Enjoy your shooting-star status and take a moment to nourish your spiritual side so business can flourish. New insights into how you operate can help implement cost-effective changes. Opportunities for lucrative partnerships are on the way, so get your affairs ready.

IF PULLED IN LOW VIBE · If you're still in the thick of the storm or recuperating from it, The Star is a reminder to look forward rather than back; to set down some of your burden rather than carrying it around like luggage. The worst has passed, so keep the faith: there is a new path opening up in front of you. This is an ideal time to heal with therapy and develop new self-soothing skills that'll help shape and usher in the life you crave. My personal mantra: "I release this anxiety and send it to someone who needs it." Healing begins when stagnant energy is released.

······

I misplaced my mojo after my brother Roc's death. I mean I could not find it anywhere—it wasn't under the seat cushion, and it wasn't under the bed. On top of my grief, my show was canceled, and acting work was getting harder to come by for a middle-aged chick.

In the midst of all this, I was having six-week-long periods and had to pee every fifteen minutes. I was in a fair amount of pain when I walked, and my stomach was rock hard. You know that weepy emotional swell you get in the few days before your cycle when you see a Hallmark commercial? I felt like that 24/7. I could barely leave the house.

I went to a doctor and told him I was crying all the time. He sent me to a shrink, who put me on Lexapro, Klonopin, and Xanax. I lost a lot of time and developed OCD, something I'd never exhibited before.

I was also eating nonstop. My appetite was devouring my identity. One day, as I sat on the couch, I felt myself spread out across the entire sofa, the entire room, and it seemed I might engulf the planet. In that moment, I left my body and shot up to the ceiling. From above, I saw I was a little tiny thing, buried in a casing of adipose and pill reliance. I feared I was slipping away for good.

My doctor told me I should have surgery for the fibroids I'd had since my early twenties. I'd never had a major surgery and said nope. I was completely focused on my rapidly deteriorating mental state. My off-balance mind felt underwater, like the spark inside me had abandoned me, or at the very least gone for a long nap.

Things came to a head when I took a trip to New York. I could barely walk a city block without stopping to catch my breath, less from the weight than the growing fibroids impinging on my organs. They were causing sporadic bouts of intense pain when they were actively growing. Maybe it was the East Coast energy, but something finally clicked in my head, and I knew I had to wake up.

When I got back to LA, I took a weekend to wean myself off all the meds cold turkey, something I don't advise, and dealt with my medical condition. Turns out, I had been suffering from an incredible hormone imbalance, with an abundance of estrogen and very little progesterone to balance it out. This had been causing my brain fog and mood swings. All my life I'd been told my fibroids were no big deal, and now I was learning they were a symptom of a greater problem. No doctor had ever even thought to check my hormones; it was a nurse practitioner who finally told me I should do so.

I was angry for a while that the medical community could fail women so miserably. But at the same time, I was happy to finally have answers and a path forward.

Black women have always had a complicated history with their reproductive organs. Surely our collective unconscious contains the trauma a slave woman must have felt toward her own body, knowing she was producing a child she loved, and also a slave. The Star encourages all women to get in touch with their root chakra, to release judgment, stagnation, and trauma to make room for healing.

18 The Moon

HIGH VIBE · Intuition, psychic ability, dream states, creativity, secrets, psyche, lucidity

LOW VIBE · Depression, delusion, lunacy, fear, isolation, addiction, anxiety, deception

The Moon represents a fertile time to journey into the liminal space that exists in between conscious and unconscious awareness.

Things may not feel completely rational or coherent at this time. Just out of view where you cannot quite see it, something's rustling in the shadows (metaphorically). Tremendous spiritual and creative clarity is possible for those willing to brave the dark unknown.

Under the light of The Moon stands The Tower (page 122), replete and duplicated. A dog and a wolf howl, the tame and wild sides of our animalistic nature. The water is human consciousness becoming conscious. Traditionally, there's a lobster at the bottom of the card, but I've used amoebas to symbolize mankind crawling out of the primordial ooze and becoming conscious by the light of the moon. The stream between the water and the pyramid is the path to enlightenment, unconscious becoming conscious. The pyramid represents mysteries revealed under The Moon's light.

You may be receiving downloads from your higher self, opening up your third eye and intuitive insights. Inner psyche work reveals secrets, dispels illusions, and helps uncover buried personal truths and mysteries. The veil between worlds is thin; psychic activity may be at a high; premonitions, lucid dreaming, and astral projection can be experienced. Keep a journal bedside to jot down your dreams.

The etheric Moon energy can feel unnerving when it shines on you. The Moon controls the ocean's tides and keeps Earth stable in its rotation; its influence is *not* to be underestimated. Can you face your true self and survive with lucidity intact? Don't stay and howl too long, lest you wander off-path permanently. Who you are, where you are from, and where you are heading: These are only some of the mysteries to unravel.

For some who pull the Moon card, recent confusion has lifted, and your senses may feel tingly and flush with creativity. Let your imaginative side out to give your higher self a voice.

In relationship dynamics, an intense connection may feel broody and moody. Communicate in new ways to open up. Others may discover there's more to a new partner than meets the eye; get all the details before handing over your heart. Check in with how you vibrate around certain people, places, and things, and spend your valuable time with what and who uplifts you.

In professional life, get all crucial data before making decisions. It's easy to misinterpret information and actions, so thoroughly check all details, vet any future prospects, use gut intuition when needed, and keep decisions, financial or otherwise, grounded in reality. This is not the time to get lost in dreams and schemes.

IF PULLED IN LOW VIBE · Darkness often reveals what daylight would hide from us. Dealing with our low-vibe shadow self can be confusing, scary, and isolating. Feelings of guilt, shame, and issues with self-esteem can cause a desire to zone out, with drugs or distractions, both of which cloud judgment. Channel yourself into studies you've been putting off, esoteric or otherwise. Your psychic abilities want to be explored; rituals, like setting up an altar, can help you unlock connections to your spirit guides. Depression, insomnia, anxiety, and, for some, mental and physical ailments can plague those trapped in The Moon's low vibration. This is the time to ask for help, if needed.

· · · · · ·

When I was a child living in the East Village, the door to the room I shared with my brother was an intricate stained-glass masterpiece, an antique from my father's shop. At night, while the light from the kitchen shone through, I would lie in frozen dread, watching roaches, in numbers too large to ignore, scuttle across the colorfully illuminated panes.

That bedroom is where I began battling with sleep paralysis, sometimes called night terrors. I'd lie in bed, feeling wide awake but not able to move; not an eyeball twitch, not a finger, not even a whisper. In my head I'd scream, *Wake up! Wake up!* It never worked. Bedtime was not about rest and recuperation; it was a time of fear and helplessness.

The trick, I learned, like most things in life, was to relax. To do so, I created meticulously curated fantasy worlds under the moon's light. Some of my best friends and favorite adventures existed only inside my head. On the surface this seems ridiculous and makes me sound like a very specific and odd child. But self-care can come in many forms!

My schoolmate Anita had similar sleep issues. Anita was the tallest, smartest girl in my class, but she lived in a studio apartment with her parents, older siblings, one niece, and one aunt. She had precious few moments of alone time except after the sun went down, too precious a stretch of time to waste on sleep.

Under the moonlight, our way to shut out the day was to roam our respective fantasy worlds, often revolving around actors we found attractive. My scenario usually went something like this: I'd run away from home and bump into The Monkees. Their silly, music-filled sitcom was on in repeats during the afternoon, and we were obsessed. I'd run into the boys on the road, and the Monkee I was least attracted to, Micky Dolenz, would adopt me. In Anita-land, Peter Tork was always her new dad. I'd enter the situation as my kid self but then rapidly age until I was old enough to marry the Monkee of my choice, which, it shouldn't surprise anybody who was a swoon-susceptible heterosexual girl at the time, was Davy Jones.

Anita and I would spend lunchtime updating each other on the previous night's adopted-groupie exploits.

"Have you heard this song by David Bowie called 'Golden Years'?" Anita breathlessly announced one day over our sandwiches. "It's sooo good. Also, Micky and I flew on the Concorde last night to Morocco for a show. It was madness."

"Morocco sounds fun," I yawned, less from feigned one-upmanship than actual lack of sleep. "Davy and I went to Pleasant Valley and picked flowers. Just him and me, so sweet. Anyway, does that song go 'what what what'? My brother won't stop playing 'Fat Bottomed Girls' when I try and use the stereo."

My nightly guardians weren't all of the boy band variety. Some nights I was adopted by Gamara, the radioactive flying Japanese turtle. Other times I pretended the zoned-out lead character from the late-night soap satire *Mary Hartman, Mary Hartman* was my very weird mother. I became Holly, the daughter from the family-among-dinosaurs series *Land of the Lost*, and traveled the stars in a rocket with Ruth Buzzi and Jim Nabors, the stars of another cheesy show, *The Lost Saucer*, which featured a weird dog-horse hybrid called a Dorse, whose needs I tended to lovingly. Mostly, though, I loved Saturday-morning TV shows like *Shazam!* and *Isis*.

I wasn't always careful about when the reveries would happen, and sometimes they'd slip out during daylight. For a time, I changed my running gait to simulate riding an Arabian horse, or even being one. I galloped away when kids called me the N-word.

Maria, the tough leader of the tightly knit Puerto Rican girl clique (most of whom were also named Maria), caught me spinning in the girls' bathroom, chanting, "Oh, mighty Isis." She demanded I meet her at lunch so she could beat me up. I politely declined, and Maria never pressed it, or told the other girls I was a would-be Egyptian goddess.

The year before, The Marias had come to my friend Anita and me with the intriguing disclosure that Satan was visiting them at night—Satan!—and gifting them things. They'd made altars and whispered convocations to the Dark Lord in a mix of Santería and Catholicism, and now their fervent prayers were being answered, and, oh, by the way, did we want in on some of the action?

"He'll give you whatever you want if you give him your soul," said one Maria.

"And marry him," giggled another.

Even then, Anita and I knew this opportunity was over our pay grade, and promptly went back to discussing bands that were not disco, with lead singers we wanted to grow up with and then marry. I'll keep Davy Jones, and my soul intact, thank you very much.

Since then I have taken back the night, and made peace with it, though I've been an insomniac ever since. Dusk to dawn has become my safety zone; it is guaranteed me time. It helps that I no longer have to fight off roaches, but what also helped was digging into my imagination. Essentially, daydreaming is creative visualization, and it allowed me to explore my subconscious desires, examine my secrets, and visualize things into reality. My flights of fancy were a soothing mechanism I was later able to make a career out of.

Before auditioning, while doing my makeup, I visualize the process: I see how fabulous the meeting will go, feel the great vibe in the room, and imagine the impact of my performance. This is precisely what I did as a kid, only now it's with a single-mindedness on manifestation rather than unfocused escapism.

The ability to shift my reality helps me grit through the semiregular dark nights of the soul that seem to make up a good chunk of human existence. My moonlit inward mind travels continue to shape my out-ward imaginative nature. They help introverted me live an occasionally extroverted life. The trick is to not get lost in illusion, disengaged from the real world. Luckily for me, this is mostly solved by being an actor, by which I'm paid to play make-believe. Not a bad gig, turning dreams into waking actualities.

19 The Sun

HIGH VIBE · Joy, lightness, optimism, expansion, wonder, happiness, freedom, growth, abundance

LOW VIBE · Lack of faith, lack of vision, self-centeredness, confusion, impulsivity, depression

The Sun is a joyous card: good things are coming or have already arrived. Accomplishments of all sorts and a new infusion of optimism ring in a celebratory energy. The Sun's reach is far and wide; life on our planet would not exist today without its nourishing rays.

Your personal magnetism is beaming out at an all-time-high frequency; others will be flocking to you. Rediscover your sense of play and reengage with the world. Laud any recent gains, even the small ones, and prepare for more.

You may have a childlike sense of wonder about the world around you. The Sun asks you to shine a light on behaviors and habits impeding growth. When you have the courage, The Sun provides a transport to happier days and greener pastures. Without The Sun's energy, the planet and its abundances would cease to exist. Don't sleep on ripe-for-the-picking, dream-fulfilling opportunities tailored for you.

In relationship dynamics, social invitations keep the calendar busy, and joyous connections mean positive vibes are abundantly flowing. For some, children might be on the way. Others are more integrated than ever with their partners and are ready to take their romantic relationship to a deeper level. Some singles feel their mojo rising, and begin to date after a break, attracting any possible number of suitors.

In professional life, some are experiencing tremendous success, new partnerships, or long-awaited career milestones. Others need to revamp their social media presence and résumé; lucrative clients and mentors can pop up unexpectedly. For others, if a particular situation doesn't work out, consider it a blessing and move on to the next thing, which might just propel you miles ahead of the pack.

IF PULLED IN LOW VIBE · No matter how dark your "dark night of the soul" gets, the dawn always comes and brings hope with it. You may feel your power is dimmed in the universe; it's not, but it does need a dusting off so you can shine on. There can be a lack of faith after recent setbacks, or childhood wounds may trigger low self-esteem, depression, and a lack of motivation, creating feelings of isolation and hopelessness.

For others, childish exuberance manifests as immaturity, self-centeredness, and a controlling nature. The world doesn't revolve around you. Shine a light on yourself before others consider you a black hole sucking the life out of the party. The temperature's perfect, the grass is green, the flowers are blooming, and the pool is heated. Climb on through the window of your bright new future and into the sunshine.

. . . . . .

When The Sun shines on you, it is a glorious thing.

A pilot called *Half & Half*, originally written for Janeane Garofalo, was now being cast with a black family. The producers wanted me to audition for the lead role of Mona Thorne.

It was pilot season, the frantic rush time of year in Los Angeles when new TV shows are cast. When the script arrived, I'd been crying over my last acting rejection. I read it quickly, giggling aloud a few times, something I didn't often do when reading sitcom scripts.

Mona was an awkward bohemian alterna chick, who would now be an awkward bohemian alterna *black* chick. I liked the idea of that. This was a character of color who wouldn't normally be seen on TV, let alone playing the lead role. Mona was the product of a divorced household and seemed to have to rely on herself rather than on her family. We had that in common. And like Mona, I had a neighbor downstairs who was a long-term friend harboring a crush on me, *and* I had a gorgeous "high yellow" sister who got more attention. It seemed like I'd lived this character already.

I made a calculated decision not to grind the comedy to dust by overrehearsing, like I normally did.

They'd tested other girls for Mona, but the network hadn't felt they could carry the show. I wondered if I could, the weight of the world on my hunched shoulders as I walked into the CBS building on Beverly Boulevard in Los Angeles. I was called into a room that might've been small, but to me it looked like a Roman amphitheater. Les Moonves, then the head of CBS, was sitting in front of me, emanating strong Emperor energy (ahem). I touched the rose quartz in my pocket, took a deep breath, and reminded myself that I was a show pony and this was my ring. Here was my chance to perform and become Mona Thorne.

Somehow, I booked the role, the leading role, and I was ecstatic, then quickly petrified. I was number one on the call sheet, and in every single scene. All eyes were on my every move. There were costume fittings, dance lessons, and a cabal of network executives with differing opinions.

Booking a series that could run for years, keep you working for years, is an actor's dream. When you book any major job in Hollywood, the heavens open up, the sun's glory shines down, you are bathed, massaged, and anointed with fine oils and butters, worshipped from near and afar, and paid handsomely. Everyone is nice to you when you're on TV, and some of them even mean it.

The joy of paying off my student loan debt alone was indicative of the Sun card's happy dynamic, but as an actor, I found some of the most delicious Sun-laden moments of having a TV show were the precious few weeks shooting the first few episodes of the season, before the show debuted. I was in a bubble playground, where my only job was to show up on time, play with my fellow actors, and hopefully create a character that resonated with an audience. There were no reviews yet, no comments on my acting, weight, or face. This is a gift I would wish for anyone, the security of knowing you're getting paid a lot of money to do what you'd probably do for free.

After the show aired, the sun beamed down again with a back nine order, and then a full season pickup of twenty-two episodes. This meant I had the freedom to create a character over the course of years, a luxury I'd never had before. Stage 14 in Studio City, California, became my home away from home and a place to experience the kind of idealized mother-daughter relationship you only see on television. Mona and her mother, Phyllis (played by Telma Hopkins), shared a bond that was foreign to me and fun to explore.

During its run, *Half & Half* was one of the top shows on UPN. I was nominated for an NAACP award for Lead Actress in a Comedy. Prince performed at the ceremony and was so good. Smokey Robinson told me he and his wife loved my show.

I really knew I had come full circle from my early days, working as a stand-in at *The Cosby Show*, when I introduced myself to my very own stand-in for *Half & Half*.

While I was basking in The Sun's glow, its bright light also revealed deeper conundrums. My father was already ill early in the show's run. On his deathbed, he badgered me to tell him about my salary, which I'd long tried not to discuss with him. Finally, I told him, expecting some kind of compliment, or maybe a fatherly warning to "invest wisely." Instead, so close to his own death, where the mask of personality lifts and the veil between worlds is thin, my white father said, "Don't spend your money nigger rich." His desiccated, paper-thin skin and lips appeared translucent as they formed the hard *R*. This was not a word we ever said in my house, so its use at this moment was unexpected.

I'd long understood my father to be a challenging and at times selfish man. Had he used this word at this moment to quell any pride I had over my salary? I knew in that moment that I had to kill and release the part of my ego and brain that might internalize this or take it to mean anything deeper about me. This was a man at the end of his time, as scared as anyone facing their own mortality. It was a late-in-life revealing moment for him, a defining moment for both of us, but not a new tragic mulatto definition of me. I knew better than to internalize or take this to mean anything deeper about me as a person, or as a person of color.

When I wrapped *Half & Half*, or *The Craft*, or *Half Baked*, it never occurred to me that years later, young women of all colors and shades would come up to me and tell me how much it meant to see someone who looked like them, that I had made them feel okay to be the weird alterna black girl magic chick they were. This truly makes me appreciate what I've accomplished.

20 Judgment

HIGH VIBE · **Resurrection, healing, clarity, revelations, spirituality, rebirth, secrets revealed, transformation**

LOW VIBE · **Denial, bad choices, lack of purpose, fear, anxiety, stagnation**

Judgment signifies a time of transformative healing.

Under the watchful eye of the angel Gabriel, figures stand with arms outstretched, signifying a release from old burdens, self-judgment, and secrets from the past. Buried memories, feuds, or resentments may come to light, for the betterment of all involved. For some, this may be a small adjustment shift; for others, their world is cracked open. Either way, your active participation is required to build a better you.

Some who pull the Judgment card may experience spiritual enlightenment, having released the pain of old burdens and disappointments. Forgiveness of yourself and others will clear a path to happiness. If life's feeling lighter, it's a testament to your past efforts to center and find balance.

Judgment and the Justice card (page 97) have a common core, but the Justice card is a somewhat passive reaction to good or bad circumstances. In Judgment, your full engagement is required in releasing and clearing out old triggers. The ability to shift out negativity is available: this is your opportunity to scrape off any remaining bits of mud clinging to your boots.

In relationship dynamics, past lovers and old friends may return for reconciliation or closure. For some, secrets swept under the rug may come up; air out what's been creating distance. Absolve yourself and show forgiveness for others. Some may find clarity from the truth and strengthen a union. Others may not like what's uncovered and make a decision to part ways.

In professional life, compete fairly and justly for what you believe, and trust your dedication is about to pay off. You may be nearing the end of a major effort or cycle. Big decisions are at hand; hear out opinions before casting judgment. Past errors may come up; be accountable and take the time to rectify your transgressions.

IF PULLED IN LOW VIBE · The Judgment card is a reminder to be an active participant in your life. You may need a change of scenery or to make a decision you've put off. Denial of present circumstances may prevent you from releasing stored unconscious emotions and pain. Intense judgment of self and others creates discord and hurt feelings and is a clear indicator that you are insecure about yourself. It's time to quell your negative inner anxiety voice and honor your responsibility to self. Examine and release old burdens like shame and self-doubt. This is your invitation to grow.

. . . . . .

Negative body image and struggles with emotional eating plagued me most of my life. I was trapped in an endless cycle of dieting, then binge eating my weight in baked goods. Whatever weight I'd lost from dieting would be gained back, plus some.

We aren't born with negative views of ourselves, nor the desire to satiate and navigate emotional issues via food. When had this set into my psyche?

Occasionally, while living with my temporary foster parents, Oma and Opa, as punishment for not finishing my dinner, I'd sit alone in the dark at the dinner table, cleared save for my plate. My mouth would be too overstuffed with food and rage to swallow. If I had to pinpoint the parturition of my emotional-eating battles, that'd be it. I would sit there, engulfed in conflicting emotions; even then, I felt I was supposed to be somewhere else, doing something else, possibly *being* someone else. In the scheme of foster care setups, I'd landed in a pretty great spot, especially considering my father had found Oma and Opa's number in an ad in the back of the newspaper. These were kind people; they just wanted me to understand how important it was to appreciate what I had. They weren't purposefully creating my eating disorders.

In high school, I developed "American girl bulimia"—that's when you're not really bulimic but aren't against throwing up once in a while. I'd binge eat, gain weight, and then hear the voice of a friend saying, "Why don't you just throw up? It's an easy way to stay skinny." So I would. This tended to leave my face bloated. I lost a few teeth, and somehow I'd still manage to gain weight, just not as much. Before I'd flush the regurgitated mess, I'd marvel at the sheer amount of money and food I was wasting. Oma and Opa's lesson had backfired.

In my twenties, there was no lover as constant, strong, and faithful as a box of chocolate-covered doughnuts. The sugar was wrecking me. I once went on a diet of only Rolos. When my blood was taken for tests, the nurse said it was like glue. My joints ached tremendously, but I hadn't put it together yet that what I was putting in my body was affecting my looks, energy, frequency, and vibration.

I'd done guided meditations with therapists before, where I'd visit my younger self. These felt downright silly, but one day I started the meditation at home and felt like I'd slipped through time. I could see my younger self, and for the first time, she could see me. It was a surreal experience, and when it was done, I realized I needed to stop judging my younger self and instead thank her for developing a coping skill on her own. I needed to release the feelings of resentment I carried before I could begin setting a new pattern.

Processing my emotions healthily was something I had to learn by going to therapy and piecing together why I'd developed this method of self-soothing. It wasn't until I did this that I was able to start making better choices. When it came down to it, I ate out of fear, loneliness, and boredom. Sweets felt like a hug. I began recognizing the difference between hunger and fear. I realized that every time I'd gotten down to Hollywood thin, I'd attracted more attention than I was comfortable with. Onstage in a character, I loved eyes on me; in real life, the gazes and people's negative comments made me feel vulnerable. Maybe I felt more comfortable at my usual ten to twenty pounds overweight because it desexualized me in the eyes of men and Hollywood.

My gyno ran a genetic panel and, unlike people who thrive on a fat-filled keto diet, my genetics said if I had more than eighteen grams of saturated fat a day, I would be overweight. This explained how I'd managed to gain five pounds eating a bag of cashews. And I no longer wondered why some people can eat a whole box of doughnuts and stay slim, while I eat just one and wear it around my waist forever.

I began to pay attention to how I felt about an hour after I ate something; if I felt sluggish and low energy, the food had to go. Thus went my beloved semiregular dinner of crackers and a brick of cheese. In the end, the fatty, savory, salty yum was not as important as my need to feel good in my body. I decided to give up dairy completely.

I quit smoking, something I had threatened to do on two previous major birthdays and in several New Year's resolutions, but hadn't been able to pull off. It felt like I'd been awakened, and the choice was to quit or resign myself to dying of cancer like my father did at sixty-one. The next time I bought a pack of cigarettes, as I slid my money across the counter, I said to myself, *I am paying someone to kill me*. I was only able to buy one more pack after this. Accepting and understanding that

I was actively engaged in the deterioration of my body empowered me to make the change.

I forgave myself for being fallible, and developed hobbies to distract myself from eating. Whenever I wanted to binge, I made a collage. I art therapied my way out of old patterns and bad habits and surprised myself one day when I turned down a piece of cake because I knew it would make me feel low vibration. These changes didn't happen immediately, but they happened sooner than I'd have assumed. Retraining my brain wasn't that hard but did require me to not bullshit myself about the real causes and effects of my actions. As a result, I felt lighter emotionally and physically.

I delved into writing, something I'd always wanted to explore, and wrote a few wobbly scripts and then a pretty good one. I started to work again, acting-wise, but nowhere near where it had been before, though I no longer lived in resentment. I started a health-centric blog to share some of the information I'd learned on my journey that I hoped could prevent other women from going through the lack of information I'd been met with. I thought to myself, "I really like writing; maybe someone will see my writing and want me to write more"—a statement I manifested as I typed these words.

Judgment requires us to look at parts of ourselves we're less than proud of. Sometimes I still go back and visit that little girl and remind her not to bite off more than she can chew, and if she does, I tell her she doesn't have to swallow anything she doesn't want to, then or ever.

21 The World

**HIGH VIBE · Completion, fruition,
happiness, graduation, closure, achievement,
accomplishment, endings**

**LOW VIBE · Loss, failure, sadness, stagnation,
hopelessness, depression, abandonment**

The World signifies the completion of The Fool's journey, and the turning of The Wheel of Fortune (page 93). The energy of all four elements comes together in harmony. There's a sense of pride, accomplishment, and gratitude in the air for the successes you've racked up. The culmination of dreams means an ending, and also the beginning of a brand-new cycle. Take time to enjoy where you are and reflect on the quality of your choices. You are responsible for current achievements; don't let anyone tell you otherwise.

You might have to pinch yourself to believe it's all real. When you do the hard work, you get big rewards. Some are feeling whole and complete with the person they've developed into. This will continue to attract opportunity and goodwill to you and your circle. Completion can bring bittersweet emotions to the surface; honor these feelings, and then put eyes on the future.

In relationship dynamics, a recent partnership, union, or birth may complete the picture of family life you've desired. Some couples may tie the knot, while others decide their partnership has reached the end of the road. These are big, life-changing decisions that move us closer to our true purpose and soul mate.

In professional life, alliances and dealings are successful and to be celebrated. Things are working out in your favor. You may have just landed a promotion, be changing scenery or jobs, or have finished an important project. Either way, the changes to come can bring further joy and happiness. If you're still pushing forward, keep up the effort: your hard work and dedication are about to pay off, bigly.

IF PULLED IN LOW VIBE · Fear of the unknown, or an inability to let go or accept an ending, may be stopping progress. A feeling of being stuck creates low self-worth. Negative thoughts are not reality; open up your flow with physical exercise and meditation to release stagnant energy and emotions stored in the body.

If your World's feeling cramped, depressing, and without hope, it's time to reconnect with what excites you and makes you feel like you're raising the vibration of yourself and your fellow man. Moving with grace through major transitions is on the table, and you're up to the task. Whatever's moving out is for your betterment and expansion. Follow your bliss to a new you.

......

To go from a nervous, quiet girl who used books to check out and then check into a reality more to her liking, to someone writing her own book that might help others check into a new reality, is mind-blowing.

As an actor, somebody tells you where to go and what to do at all times. As a writer, I have to corral myself. I'd settle into writing from ten p.m. to three a.m. At times it felt weird, like I was living a vampiric life. The country was asleep, but I had no kids or five a.m. call times. This book gave me the freedom to enjoy my body's weird natural hours. There's tons more to do—the editing process, the design of the tarot deck, which I hope you love—but this project, while on the cusp of completion, I hope will live on.

My hope is that this book and the included cards will help you find a new piece of yourself, that you might peel back a layer and reveal the bright shiny skin underneath marred flesh. I hope you have your own epiphany, as I did, that the fear of a thing is 99 percent of the time so much worse than dealing with the thing, a process that allows you to move forward organically, as it has for me and my friends.

In studying tarot, I've gained a greater appreciation for religion and the sanctity it offers, and trust you see how tarot fits in seamlessly with any spiritual practice, regardless of designation. Tarot is, as I've always said, a way to clarify the now so you can manifest the future you want. It's not up to fate or the law of attraction completely, although it's a part, but that school of thought leaves out how important your active participation is for the desired outcome. I got up at three a.m. on two hours of sleep to drive an hour and 20 minutes for a five a.m. call time because I wanted to be an actress. I've gotten healthy in body and hopefully in mind by actively making it a goal to do so. I finished this book because I wanted it, so I wrote when I didn't feel like it and wrote even more when I did.

To have birthed something born of my passion, that's Wand energy. A deep desire to share with others what has helped me grow is Cups energy. I've given it mental focus—Sword energy—and manifested it into a tangible thing you are now holding in your hand—Discs energy. My dream is that in some small way this book might help raise the vibration of the planet. When that happens, society gets more conscious as a whole.

There's been beauty, challenges, and serendipity to this last year while writing this book, and it's amazing to walk into a new chapter of my life filled with light. As I move on to my next adventure, wherever it takes me, I am so grateful for my last chapter, for the people, places, books, and laughter.

For most artists, within every creative endeavor pulled off, there are moments of joy; bits of happiness tie-dyed with a sense of pride and accomplishment. And yet, these high-vibe emotions are more oft than not duly dipped in worry and heavily dusted with a pervasive creeping fear that this is it, the last and final job, I will never work again. There will be no new beginnings.

It's like an anxiety-fueled infinity loop of mourning the ending of a thing while simultaneously still experiencing or trying to achieve the thing. Luckily, the human mind is a fickle but generally trainable beast. Every ending affords another chance to right the wrongs and better the bests.

In the name of more healthily navigating the sense of an ending, I've learned that one of the important things to do with conclusions, desired or otherwise, is to acknowledge and feel the "watershed-ness" of said moment. Take the time to luxuriate in the fleeting waves of random happiness when goals are accomplished. Alternatively, recognize the surrendering sigh of relief when an ending to hardships and a thread of hope is finally in sight.

I do not think every terrible thing that befalls us happens for a reason. Bad things happen to good people all the time. I do think that how we handle these challenges is the true test. This means having the audacity to believe that there will be a new beginning and the comprehension that the depths of our lows—our personal nadirs—are directionally proportional to the height of one's apex and ability to fly high.

I've encountered and learned from each of the various iterations of myself on my fool's journey, and in the end, the multiplicity of selves seems to round back and unspool in an infinity loop. The only thing I'm certain will come is more endings and more beginnings, brimming with sorrow and solace, promise and pain, closure and completion.

"The privilege of a lifetime is to become who you truly are."

—Carl Jung

THE

MINOR

ARCANA

Ace of Wands

HIGH VIBE · **Creation, sexuality, rebirth, opportunity, brilliance, passion, spontaneity, confidence, intuition, fertility, ambition, talent, inspiration**

LOW VIBE · **Ego, setback, delay, fear, chaos, rage, dullness, blocked intuition, fear, sexual dysfunction**

Aces carry the potential of their whole suit—in this case, Wands. That means the potential for action, new opportunities, and new ideas!

This might mean a fiery jolt of cosmic inspiration—the opening of the mind's eye and your root chakra. You may be brimming with ideas, kinetic energy, sexual passion, and a new confidence.

In relationship dynamics, an enticing new person with invigorating energy may have appeared. Couples can get a burst of renewed passion, and possibly a pregnancy. Intense mental and sexual attraction in high vibe can elevate; in low vibe, it clouds judgment and drains energy. Remember, flames can go out quickly.

In professional life, opportunities may come and go quickly at this time. Your inspiration is percolating in a big way and can attract attention. Whether you're celebrating a win or are at the genesis of the next big thing, you have the power to become who you envision.

IF PULLED IN LOW VIBE · If you're enduring setbacks, remember they're temporary and not the truth of who you are. It's never too late to actively turn dreams into reality. You may feel dulled out, sexually frustrated, financially burdened, and/or creatively blocked. Others can feel frazzled, with a short fuse. Your personal power is much larger than you know: it's time to ignite your fire.

2 of Wands

You may feel pulled in different directions. There are a multitude of possibilities, and your focus is on the future. Travel may be in the cards as well. With so much going on, it can be easy to lose focus. Balance your desires with reality, eschew distractions, and keep your eyes on the prize.

In relationship dynamics, make sure you're on the same page as your partner, as change is in the air. You may have met an inspiring new partner. Conflicting ambitions can cause separation; some couples need to strike a balance between personal life and work.

In professional life, you may be germinating a new idea, or super focused on a project. Some are restless and impatient with the daily grind. Shake up the day to day by speaking up with concepts that could help out the whole team. This might be the time to strike out on your own.

HIGH VIBE · Options, intuition, potential, focus, choices, independence, planning, ambition

LOW VIBE · Lack of drive, low energy, imbalance, powerlessness, disconnection

You may be feeling like you can do anything and take over the world! Twos are about choice, and Wands are about action: formulate a plan and figure out the best way to turn what you covet into reality.

IF PULLED IN LOW VIBE · Without a plan, there can be a lack of confidence and waning of personal energy. Fear of the unknown or fear of failure or success may be triggering you and blocking your energy. If you're feeling bogged down, overwhelmed, and depleted, turn your efforts to what's within your control rather than lamenting what isn't.

3 of Wands

HIGH VIBE · **Hope, confidence, success, planning, vision, inspiration, expansion, opportunity, freedom, effort**

LOW VIBE · **Disappointment, frustration, dullness, poor planning, separation, apathy, dejection, stagnation, lack of patience, setback**

Having experienced a few gains and missteps, you're more prepared, and have a better understanding of your place in the world. That should be freeing, not constraining. Contemplate before you strike out on your next big venture. Now you know it's important to curate a plan, rather than act on blind luck or misguided faith.

There's a synergistic energy around you; things are coming to fruition. The birds represent ideas in action. The figure in the card sits above the water; they aren't bogged down by their emotions. This allows them to focus on growth and expansion.

Some may be losing interest in a current situation, with wanderlust in the air. Your eyes and heart are on the unknown. Travel may be on the agenda. Others may have done the work and are waiting for their ships to come in. Your personal power and determination can propel you closer to goals: follow your inner convictions.

In relationship dynamics, there may be an upcoming date or event on the horizon. Others may be keeping it casual with a plethora of choices at their disposal. There can be a transient nature to relationships: clear communication is key.

In professional life, rapid growth is available. Opportunities might not fall in your lap, so be diligent in pursuing all leads. This is an auspicious time for planting seeds.

IF PULLED IN LOW VIBE · There may be confusion and lack of direction. You need to open up your tunnel vision to the great wide world of opportunities available. Don't let fear and self-doubt get the best of you. Plan, prepare, and claim your future success.

4 of Wands

can stand the test of time, if it's built on a solid foundation.

Some may be energized, having found their tribe in a new group of friends or a work situation. A sense of community tunes the frequency to a lighter, happier station. Stability and comfort lead to upcoming milestones, making this a seminal time. Enjoy the good vibes.

In relationship dynamics, this can be considered a card of marriage, or might come up when you're on the verge of an important union of any sort. Taking dynamics to a new, deeper level brings some partners closer. Singles may find that this is the perfect time to mingle.

In professional life, a big deal might've just closed, or other reasons to celebrate are at hand. Your inviting demeanor and creative solutions get others to support your goals. People are noticing your magnetic energy and passionate drive.

HIGH VIBE · **Security, stability, confidence, success, harmony, celebration, graduation, fulfillment**

LOW VIBE · **Unproductive partnership, mistrust, low confidence, instability, loss of power, change of the status quo, rejection, dispersed energy**

A joyful feeling in the air brushes away the doldrums and lifts spirits. It's a festive time of goodwill, community, and celebration. You may be feeling centered and confident in your choices. What you create and synthesize now

IF PULLED IN LOW VIBE · If you haven't quite reached your goals, keep up the hard work; trust that you're creating your future. Check in on how you feel energetically around people close to you. Do they make you vibrate higher or lower? If you're feeling on shaky ground or there's discord at home, take accountability and action toward creating your vision of happiness.

5 of Wands

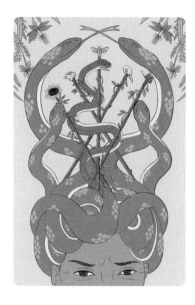

HIGH VIBE · **Creativity, collaboration, playful energy, physical expression, release of energy**

LOW VIBE · **Competition, aggression, defensiveness, conflict, isolation, aggressiveness, friction, jealousy, envy**

Friendly competition and competitive play can help you grow. Competition may sound negative, but this is a time of being around equally qualified creative or talented people who spur you on to greater heights. Having someone who pushes you is good for you, whether you're athletes or Salieri and Mozart. A rapid-fire exchange of ideas creates active energy, propelling everyone forward.

In relationship dynamics, a fun, feisty, sexy energy may be felt. Passion can quickly dissolve into discord if words and tone are not considered. Be aware of communication styles. If you've met someone new, get all the facts: occasionally the 5 of Wands can mean one or both parties are playing the field.

In professional (or personal) life, when a lightbulb moment hits, don't put it on hold. It's out there in the ether, and someone else might claim it for their own if you don't. Challenging dynamics can bring the team down; focus on your own gifts and strengths.

IF PULLED IN LOW VIBE · Gossiping and envy will only slow your roll. Engaging in unnecessary struggles or conflicts or, alternatively, isolating yourself means you're living in the low vibe. Issues around low self-esteem or low self-worth may be coming up. Wands are cards of action, and how much energy you're willing to put into reconnecting with yourself and others is the question at hand. Can you rise above the fray and tap into your personal power? Show everyone who you really are.

6 of Wands

HIGH VIBE · **Achievement, confidence, accolades, success, power, recognition, optimism, victory**

LOW VIBE · **Failure, disappointment, narcissism, hubris, insecurity, self-centeredness, hollow victory**

A recent victory, won by your strength, drive, and determination, has brought success. The recent accolades are well deserved. It's time to accept the recognition and praise of others. If victory is not yet at hand, this is the time to galvanize.

In relationship dynamics, you may have your pick, as well as be attracting a new caliber of person. There's a sense of pride and a tad of ego to this card—don't let it get the best of you! Some couples may be celebrating news that affects both parties.

In professional life, you may be riding high on a big success, and your talents are shining. This a card of personal triumph; if you aren't there yet, remain diligent and committed to your plan of action. Success is near, and others are paying close attention to your efforts, awaiting big results.

IF PULLED IN LOW VIBE · There may be an overwhelming sense of hubris and a need for others to prop up the ego. Real or imagined failures may have gotten the best of you, creating a lack of drive, depression, envy, and/or jealousy. If you're slipping into low-vibe behavior it's a good time to back up and refocus on your goals, rather than fixate on things that haven't worked out in your favor.

7 of Wands

In relationship dynamics, strong-willed, passionate individuals who don't easily compromise may be coming together. For some, it can indicate a hot-and-cold dynamic. Get to the real issue rather than circling around it. You're more powerful when you work together.

In professional life, you may be pitching new ideas or outside-the-box concepts to people who don't yet see your vision. Your talent and take-charge attitude can win people over to your way of thinking, despite naysayers. To defuse in-house power struggles, give others a fair say, even if you think they're wrong.

HIGH VIBE · Inner conviction, defending honor, confidence, power, pride, assertion, resilience

LOW VIBE · Defeat, rivalry, instability, opposition, defensiveness, anger, struggle

There may be some challenges coming your way. Stand up and defend your beliefs, ideas, and inner convictions. There may be friction in the air, but you can handle it in a high-vibe way. Others may try to throw you off balance; keep your footing.

IF PULLED IN LOW VIBE · When we feel misunderstood and not in our power, it's easy to be defensive and cut people off and out of our lives. Defending yourself from real or imagined enemies can be exhausting; focus on the tasks at hand while learning to communicate your needs more effectively. When tempers flare, examination of anger and control issues may be needed in order for you to move more efficiently through life. Isolation and feelings of victimization can overwhelm if left unchecked. This is your time to believe in yourself. Don't get mad—get motivated.

8 of Wands

HIGH VIBE · **Growth, power, new opportunities, forward movement, focus, psychic messages, advancement, intuition**

LOW VIBE · **Lack of drive, laziness, dullness, depression, scattered energy, low libido, aloofness**

If you pull this card, it's a great time to actively take the steps needed to accomplish what you want. It can also represent psychic energy; your mental projections and thoughts can manifest into real-world results, so be clear about what you're calling in.

A combination of old-school hitting the pavement and constructive creative visualization is ideal for manifesting what you want. Your inner life-force energy carries tremendous power when focused and projected out into the world with purpose. This is an auspicious time to tap into available intuitive energy. Quick-coming bits of information and opportunities can come and go just as easily. Carpe diem!

In relationship dynamics, Cupid's bow is aimed squarely at you, and this can be an exhilarating time for the senses. People may be magnetically drawn to you. If single, reach out directly or send some mental energy toward a crush and watch the sparks fly. Be aware that for some, a rush of intensity may dissipate quickly—better options are on the way.

In professional life, remain focused on the task at hand. Talk is cheap—show people with action rather than words, and they'll be doubly impressed.

IF PULLED IN LOW VIBE · Your personal power is waiting to be turned on. Laser-precision focus is needed to move forward. That means letting go of distractions that let you check out and disengage. For some, depression, anxiety, or mania may be present and need addressing.

9 of Wands

HIGH VIBE · Perseverance, tenacity, grit, fortitude, determination, mental clarity, obligation, duty

LOW VIBE · Exhaustion, lack of motivation, sorrow, mental trauma, anxiety, defensiveness

Achieving great heights requires tenacity, drive, and grit. You may be tirelessly grinding or up against a difficult situation: trust that you've got the stamina to persevere and succeed. Stay the course, even if you feel like a wounded warrior.

You've put in a lot of effort to get to this point, and may be wondering if you'll ever see results. This is a common feeling right before a big win. There's one last mountain to climb, and the rewards are just on the other side.

In relationship dynamics, you may need to reinvigorate your daily routine. Don't make assumptions about what your partner is thinking or throw in the towel before seeking clarity. Couples may have come through an arduous patch and now feel more connected. Any relationship that stands the test of time will go through ups and downs. For some, effort may be needed to renew connections and see if attraction is still present. Patience and active communication rather than fatalism will pave the way.

In professional life, you may be burning the midnight oil and feeling bone weary. The payoff is closer than you think. Stakes are high; tap into your reserve tank to accomplish goals and meet deadlines. If overburdened, delegate some responsibilities and things will run smoother.

IF PULLED IN LOW VIBE · Exhaustion, anxiety, and a defeatist attitude can have you spinning your wheels. Some may need a break to regroup. If you realize you're the low-vibe force in your social circle or relationship, this is a moment of adjustment.

10 of Wands

HIGH VIBE · **Completion, fortitude, grit, determination, accomplishment, release of burdens**

LOW VIBE · **Exhaustion, end of rope, loss of faith, depletion, struggle, negativity**

Bringing projects to fruition is rewarding but can make you feel like the weight of the world is on your shoulders. Set down any loads that aren't yours to carry. If you've recently completed a major endeavor, it's time to rest and rejuvenate. If not, stay the course and you'll see hard work pay off. Dynamics may be culminating; take a look at what's ready for harvest and what never bloomed. This is the final push, a dig-deep moment.

In relationship dynamics, things may feel a bit heavy. Both parties may be tired and exhausted; let go of old arguments and stop struggling against what has already happened. For some, the connection has run its course. This can be challenging to process, but surrender may bring emotional relief.

In professional life, projects may be coming to completion and responsibilities may be weighing on you. You're up to the task, and success is in sight. If you're overwhelmed, ask for help rather than micromanaging. Examine patterns and how they contribute to current success or missteps.

IF PULLED IN LOW VIBE · When energy is scattered, it's difficult to focus and almost impossible to manifest. Is the right move to carry on with a stiff upper lip, or to let go and cut your losses? Holding on to demanding and demeaning situations that may already be over will zap your energy. Struggling through a "dark night of the soul" and loss of faith can ultimately lead us to spiritual enlightenment. This is an opportunity to course correct and attain what you desire.

Princess of Wands

HIGH VIBE · **Attraction, beginnings, messages, optimism, freedom, focus, ambition, burgeoning sexuality**

LOW VIBE · **Suppressed energy, lethargy, inertia, mania, procrastination**

This Princess signifies beginning to understand how to utilize and harness your personal energy, creativity, and sexual power. They're the charismatic extrovert who's always got a great tale or shows up to whisk you off on an adventure. Often the center of attention, they're willing to share the spotlight and encourage others to shine (when they're in high vibe, at least).

This card may represent someone exploring a new path and becoming aware of new opportunities. They may be setting off on their own for the first time or the hundredth time. This Princess explores where their talents lie and may be starting a new project or acquiring a new skill set. More so than the other Princesses, the Princess of Wands is also learning to harness their sexuality. This can be done in a positive way, or manipulatively. You'll learn from experience what works for you.

In relationship dynamics, this Princess is a seductress in training, and a magnetic mate. Dating can be exciting, but a little like playing with fire if you're big on commitment. The Princess of Wands can open up your world if you let them in, though their interest can wane depending on their mercurial moods. They may have eyes on more than one person at a time, so communicate your needs and be clear that you're on the same page.

In professional life, be on the lookout for new opportunities and pay attention to people with advice that may prove useful. You can pull others into your orbit with a clever mind and imaginative way of thinking, but to work in a group setting, you sometimes need to rein in your passion.

IF PULLED IN LOW VIBE · Exuberant personalities can underestimate their overwhelming effect on those around them. If this feels like you, it's time to make space for others. Self-focus can move you forward, but a desire to dominate or an intense self-centeredness can be draining.

Prince of Wands

HIGH VIBE · **Action, adventure, opportunities, exuberance, sexuality, attraction, freedom**

LOW VIBE · **Lacking energy, low drive, scattered, manic, unreliable, ego**

The Prince of Wands represents your fiery life-force energy, applied confidently in the real world. They follow their creative whims and know that passion is one of their greatest assets and can lead in the direction of a fulfilling career.

This card may signify a creative, inventive person, like Basquiat, keen for adventure and willing to take risks. If they had a motto, it would be "It's better to burn out than fade away." Intense focus and expenditure of energy are needed.

Exploring without a set plan can lead to brilliant discoveries, as well as land you in a few tricky spots. Stay driven and grounded to separate fantasy from reality. Have fun, but don't forget to focus on long-term goals. Sometimes the Prince of Wands represents a playboy/-girl party-animal type, up for any escapade thrown their way. They may come out of nowhere, draw you in with just a look, and offer what you've been craving.

In relationship dynamics, this charming, sexy suitor is sure to make you feel magical and desired. A wanderlust mentality may be present; if you're looking for commitment, make sure to communicate your needs and listen carefully to their reply.

In professional life, things can move quickly. In your excitement, don't overlook the details and fine print. It's not difficult to win others over to your way of thinking, but be sure to give them a voice. Opportunities are available when you put your best self on display. Logic and intuition are a winning combination.

IF PULLED IN LOW VIBE · You may be caught up in the moment, letting responsibilities slide. It could be burnout or apathy, or possibly motivated by jealousy. Control issues may have you erupting in anger at others. Anxiety and/or manic behavior can lead to dysfunction. You need rejuvenation. Harness your inner strength to find direction and purpose.

Queen of Wands

HIGH VIBE · Desire, will, lust, sensuality, creativity, manifestation

LOW VIBE · Lethargy, depression, self-loathing, lack of power, mania, repressed sexuality

This Queen doesn't run with the wolves—they *are* the wolf. Passionate and sensual, they possess a strong life-force energy. They're comfortable in their own skin and champion individuality.

Embracing and nourishing emotional, mental, and sexual well-being is part of their strength. Honoring personal power has gotten them far. If you pull this card, you may have had a series of well-earned successes and feel on top of your game.

If representing a maternal figure in your life, this Queen engages emotionally and energetically with their loved ones. They encourage self-expression and keep their wards scheduled with various artistic and athletic activities.

In relationship dynamics, your light is shining bright, and many moths and butterflies may be drawn. For some, a sexual liberation reconnects you to a partner, or may put you back on the dating scene. You may feel a strong attraction to a new and mysterious lover or friend after a period of dormancy. Get the full story before committing, as they may be playing the field.

In professional life, things feel electric. Your next idea may be the very thing that moves a current project forward or lands a big payday. Advocate for yourself, but don't force others to your way of thinking through aggressive behavior. This is an ideal time to send out a résumé if you're looking for work; your energy is flowing.

**IF PULLED IN LOW VIBE · Often we're taught to make others comfortable at our own expense, and we can expend energy on dead-end situations. Suppression may cause frustration, stagnation, and/or depression. When out of balance or in their ego, this Queen may become energetically overwhelming or experience intimacy issues or sexual dysfunction. They can also be a not-so-great friend, unable or unwilling to provide the same level of support they expect of others.

King of Wands

HIGH VIBE · Confidence, energetic, creative, dynamic, charismatic, inspiration, leadership

LOW VIBE · Depression, mania, low self-esteem, inflated ego, passivity, disconnection, directionless

This King represents a fascinating, action-driven individual whose exuberant energy is contagious. Persuasive with words, there's something alluring, almost dangerous, to their seductive charm; they can adapt to the energy around them and use it to their advantage.

If you pull this card, you may be manifesting something that has felt out of reach. There's momentum around you; it's a great time to meet like-minded people who inspire you.

If representing a paternal figure in your life, this spontaneous King is fully engaged and encourages others to work up to their potential, mostly through positive reinforcement. A sense of humor helps them appreciate and nurture individuality.

In relationship dynamics, a sexy, life-of-the-party charmer may have recently walked into your heart. They may prefer to play the field and be slow to commit, but once they do, they make an attentive, passionate partner. Some may be reconnecting with a current love, while others begin dating after a time-out.

In professional life, your ideas can catch on and pay off big, so be on alert for opportunities. This card may represent a boss or mentor who can provide inspiration when needed most. Maybe they have a fondness for their own voice, but there is something to glean from them.

IF PULLED IN LOW VIBE · This King may give off mixed signals, appearing flighty, unreliable, or reckless. A frenetic or manic energy may overwhelm loved ones. For some, recent disappointments may cause low energy, depression, anxiety, and a general loss of hope or faith. An intervention is needed before self-involvement or narcissistic behavior undermines your hard work.

Ace of Cups

HIGH VIBE · **Love, joy, happiness, abundance, opportunity, fertility, productivity, intuition**

LOW VIBE · **Depression, endings, break ups, unrequited feelings, rejection**

Aces carry the potential of their whole suit; in the case of Cups, that means there is an abundance of emotional satisfaction and love available—love of self and/or love of others. This is not a guarantee, but the energy is there for those who want it. When you embrace the Ace of Cups, you vibrate higher than fear, shame, or doubt. This is a perfect time to open up your heart and world,

expand horizons, and gain new perspectives. If you're not there yet, this is an opportunity to let go of what's been dragging you down and welcome in joy.

In relationship dynamics, a new interest holds the potential for real love and actual fulfillment. Couples may feel a renewed, deepening connection; singles are glowing, vibrating on a frequency that others are picking up on. Some are ready to date after heartbreak; others may end situations that are causing pain and move toward more satisfying prospects.

In professional life, a rebirth of interest or possible total reset is moving you toward your dream position. Some might have an overabundance of responsibilities: you're up to the task. Opportunities for advancement exist if you let the boss know you're a committed and dedicated member of the team.

IF PULLED IN LOW VIBE · "Woe is me," victim-y energy can repel the very things you want. The ability to attract love can be proportional to your own personal vibration. You may feel disappointed, possibly even drowning in emotions after setbacks. Check your inner dialogue. If someone else spoke to you in the same tone, would you vibrate toward them or away from them? Hypersensitization or being too self-focused can lower your vibe. When you start to value yourself, healthy love is waiting.

2 of Cups

HIGH VIBE · **Partnership, union, love, happiness, joy, cooperation, mutual attraction, reconciliation, harmony, balance**

LOW VIBE · **Codependence, rejection, separation, imbalance, one-sided attraction, isolation, discord**

An auspicious new love or partnership might have you walking on cloud nine; the tingly, exciting feeling going on is a dopamine gold mine! For some, this card heralds true love.

This is a relationship card and indicates a partnership that could go the distance. For those who have closed themselves off, when you get this card in a reading, it's an invitation to look at how you view, process, and engage in emotional and physical intimacy. For some, it's time to examine how you were taught to love as a child, and create new, healthier patterns.

In relationship dynamics, you may be awakening to a strong mutual attraction with a soul mate. Some are freshly in *love*, feeling seen and appreciated. Others are in the beginning stages of heavy "like." Enjoy the moment and resist the temptation to rush things or feelings. Singles who desire a connection should visualize their perfect partner. You have the power to manifest what you desire.

In professional life, you may have landed a dream job, an important interview, or a big contract. Things are unfolding naturally, and in your favor. Others are drawn to ideas you champion. If you're still waiting for new opportunities, keep a lookout—they're coming your way.

IF PULLED IN LOW VIBE · Rejection, one-sided attraction, or an imbalance of power may have you blue. Sometimes an instant attraction to a person, specific idea, or job creates attachment to a desired outcome. When things don't work out, disappointment can turn to depression. Examine low-vibe connections and patterns and use this time to shed old baggage. It's time to make way for new loves.

3 of Cups

HIGH VIBE · **Teamwork, friendship, abundance, pleasure, community, optimism, growth, festivities**

LOW VIBE · **Discord, overindulgence, debauchery, jealousy, isolation, stagnation, interloper, competition, distraction, aloofness**

A fun, social time, full of gatherings and celebrations, is at hand. New and intriguing people may have entered the scene, uplifting the general mood. Things should feel festive, with less stress and strife to the daily grind. Make the most of new and old connections and engage with those who uplift your vibration.

In relationship dynamics, you may be playing the field, flirting and seeing who's up to par. Some may be reuniting with old friends and lovers. For others, a child or an addition to the family may be in store. Occasionally this card can mean an interloper, a third party in a situation, so communication is key. If you're not involved, now's the time to get back out there. Be open to new experiences.

In professional life, new connections and recent developments can provide great returns now and in the future. Stay open to innovative ways of thinking; your hard work is catching the eye of those in a position to help your dreams become reality. Don't push too hard; let things flow naturally. Old clients may return in this time of abundance.

IF PULLED IN LOW VIBE · Jealousy, isolation, or depression may be causing an emotional shutdown. Rejection or recent disappointment may be getting the best of you. Petty or baseless gossip should be avoided. There's value in communing with others who support and nurture your dreams. Go out and find your true tribe.

4 of Cups

HIGH VIBE · **Self-reflection, meditation, focus, personal time-out, emotional space**

LOW VIBE · **Malaise, detachment, isolation, discontent, boredom, apathy, stubbornness**

To build a more stable foundation, your personal need for space should take precedence. You need an emotional time-out. For some, this means a break from everyone and everything demanding your time. Peace and quiet will aid in reconnecting you to your passions with a fresh perspective.

If you're already in a period of withdrawal or self-protection, this card may be telling you it's time to reconnect with the world at large. Some may give or receive an offer of friendship or love that's met with little interest. Don't take it personally if you're rejected. If the shoe is on the other foot, let the wearer down easy.

In relationship dynamics, a need for space or a redefining of boundaries may be present. Distance and aloofness can cause partners to feel left out or taken for granted. You can need space but still love someone; it doesn't mean the dynamic is over for good. All healthy relationships have ups and downs. Use this time to figure out if the goal is reconnection, or if things have run their course. Some may be ready to offer their cup of love after a dormant period.

In professional life, block out distractions and focus on the projects at hand. You may be working alone and find that boredom with the daily grind has set in. You're building your future, so stay on task and out of office politics.

IF PULLED IN LOW VIBES · A lack of motivation can create a fortress of loneliness around you. Intuition dulls when feelings of isolation take over. It's easy to get lost in the solitude of daydreams and distractions. Release fear connected to stored pain. When the need to protect yourself impedes personal growth, it's time to leave the cocoon and learn to fly.

5 of Cups

In relationship dynamics, a period of recovery after emotional upheaval or turbulence may have you feeling relief and a renewed connection to your partner. When you release sadness, you make room for an expansion of love. For some, the choice to let go of past resentments and move forward together or end things for good may be on the table, in either personal or professional relationships. Love is still available if your partnership goals are aligned.

In professional life, you may need to regroup after a setback. Some received a smaller piece of the pie than expected. Things are now moving in the right direction with the focus on what can be accomplished, rather than on what was lost. The demise of past aspirations makes way for more profitable situations to come in.

HIGH VIBE · Release, reengagement, hope, reunion, independence, closure, acceptance

LOW VIBE · Heartbreak, disappointment, grief, obsession, depression, stagnation, regret

When you're too focused on the emotional pain of what didn't work out, you miss what's still available to you. You may be in a period of processing disappointments, rejections, and/or bouts of negative thinking. A conscious choice must be made to set down burdens and baggage in order to salvage what remains.

IF PULLED IN LOW VIBE · Attempts to control situations that are no longer serving you are draining your energy. Staring too long at the past and what is already gone causes stagnation. Letting go of attachment to a desired outcome will allow new energy to flow your way. Emotional overload can leave us in a victim space. Numbing or drowning your feelings may cause depression and anxiety. Often, we wrap pain so tightly around us, it becomes a defining feature. It's time to release that pain and open yourself to new love.

6 of Cups

In relationship dynamics, some might be meeting a new soul mate or rekindling a past connection that was deeper than previously realized. Reminiscing can bring up mutual feelings, or reveal an unrequited longing. Welcome reunions with friends or family may be taking place. You're realizing how much others appreciate you.

In professional life, things should be operating smoothly between you and your client or boss. You're probably feeling valued and integral. If you're up for a job or promotion, there's a great chance the powers that be have already taken notice of you. If you're searching for the right fit, a positive, sunny disposition is paramount for attracting success.

HIGH VIBE · **Reunion, forgiveness, healing, joy, peaceful time, satisfaction, childlike wonder, nostalgia**

LOW VIBE · **Separation, anger, mistrust, pain, suffering, abandonment, low self-esteem**

There's a lot of joy to be found in simple, everyday things. A sense of innocence and freedom is elevating your vibe. Long-forgotten memories may arise. Reconnecting with the past provides answers about the present and hints at the future.

IF PULLED IN LOW VIBE · Letting go of past sorrow creates an opening for new experiences and greater love. Recent events, like a breakup or emotional loss, may have reopened old wounds, leaving you in a state of confusion or crisis. Refusing to accept the end of a partnership can cause depression and anxiety. Negative thought patterns can keep you trapped and emotionally lost in the past. Find a healthy way to express and release these emotions.

7 of Cups

to your higher self. If you're pondering an important decision, stay focused on your goals and moving forward on your path.

In relationship dynamics, you might be lost in a dreamy bubble of love. Make sure you're both on the same page, as it's easy to overlook important differences at this time. Some may have feelings for more than one person; you may need to make a choice, or the choice will be made for you.

In professional life, think outside the box while keeping an eye on details. If the stakes are high, this is not a time to hem and haw; make clear, decisive choices that prove you're an integral asset or team leader.

HIGH VIBE · **Choice, options, dream states, luxury, intuition, reflection, meditation**

LOW VIBE · **Avoidance, laziness, self-absorption, delusion, overindulgence, distraction, illusions, procrastination**

Choices and options are often accompanied by divine inspiration, as well as occasional confusion. Intuitive messages leading to clarity can happen at this time; keep a journal with you to note your epiphanies, and stay open

IF PULLED IN LOW VIBE · Daydreamland is a fun place to visit, but don't get lost drifting in malaise, or you may find yourself blindsided. Delusions, distraction, and inaction can drown out desire and ambition. Take stock of what you are wasting time on that's keeping you from attending to your and your potential partner's emotional needs. Getting lost in self-involvement and/or being inconsiderate of others' feelings can lead you to miss warning signs. It's time for a more analytical mind-set, in order to dial in to what you truly desire.

8 of Cups

HIGH VIBE · **Change, endings, journeys, strength, decisions, reconnection, hope**

LOW VIBE · **Stagnation, instability, abandonment, lack of commitment, aloofness**

Recent endings and the emotional sadness that came with them are lifting. Moving away from situations that are weighing you down will bring lightness. Release and relief are possible when the focus is shifted to the new opportunities at hand.

In relationship dynamics, you may feel like opening to new connections after a period of confusion or sadness. Walking away from a difficult situation has brought healing and clarity about what is desired in a partner. Some may decide to separate, or find that a friendship has run its course. Others are stuck on the idea of reconciling with an ex.

In professional life, this card can be a sign to walk away from dead-end situations, be they business or personal. Breakthroughs in thinking help you come up with a solution for a problem. For others, an arduous project is coming to completion. New, exciting projects and opportunities are on the horizon. The temperament of a cranky coworker may have caused problems previously, but you don't have to squabble with office politics. If you're searching for work, try new approaches or revamp your résumé.

IF PULLED IN LOW VIBE · Fulfilling connections are available when you are open to them. This is an invitation to examine attachments that are keeping you stuck in old patterns. Feelings of stagnation, abandonment, depression, and anxiety need emotional release work. Codependency may be dragging you down. Learning to self-nurture and self-soothe will help you count every inch forward as a victory. Stop looking back—opportunities are never in the rearview mirror.

9 of Cups

HIGH VIBE · **Abundance, comfort, ease, achievement, wish fulfillment, blessings, inheritance, gratitude, luxury**

LOW VIBE · **Sadness, stagnation, depression, disease, disappointment, failure**

You're feeling clear on what you desire and aware of how to attract it to you. Emotional and spiritual release work has brought a sense of well-being and tremendous personal growth. When dreams come to fruition, savor the goodwill. In some circles, the 9 of Cups is known as the wishing card:

manifest to your heart's desire—it's time to shine!

In relationship dynamics, you may be attracting a variety of viable suitors or friends. Connections to any current partners should be feeling on point, and milestones may be reached. Some may add to their family during this joyful time. If you're still searching for intimacy, emotional or physical, this is an auspicious time to attract a match into your life.

In professional life, opportunities are coming or are already available. If you're celebrating recent accomplishments, it's okay to treat yourself, if finances permit. If you're searching for work, manifesting the perfect situation is possible if you put in the legwork. Journaling and creative visualization can help facilitate your visions for the future. Imagine the steps along the way, not just the outcome.

IF PULLED IN LOW VIBE · Setbacks and disillusionment can lead to feelings of victimization and a negative outlook. Desires are within reach, although you may need a reality check before moving forward. Some may have found achieving their dreams has left a hollow feeling, where prideful haughtiness morphs into smugness. Time to get back on your path and intuit which road leads to personal happiness.

10 of Cups

HIGH VIBE · **Completion, happiness, commitment, family, emotional fulfillment, contentment, abundance**

LOW VIBE · **Turmoil, isolation, denial, attachment disorders, sadness, disconnection**

A time of joy, happiness, and completion replete with a sense of communal love is at hand. Celebrate the bounty of hard work and the culmination of your emotional desires. You may have recently graduated or experienced another major milestone. The vibe of fulfillment can carry a bittersweet note for some, as completion leads to endings. Rejoice, as new beginnings are on the way. If you're in transition, know that you are moving toward success.

In relationship dynamics, you may have met someone special or gotten married, or might be in the process of blending a family. Celebrations and gatherings are happening; savor the inner peace and enjoy the exciting revelry. If you're still searching, you could meet a potential life partner at this time.

In professional life, you may receive a promotion or raise, or a big project may be in its final stages. There may be last-minute jitters, but keep faith that the results will be well received and your participation rewarded. If you haven't seen progress yet, keep pushing—victory is close.

IF PULLED IN LOW VIBE · Feelings of depression, failure, or stagnation may be overwhelming you, creating an isolating, lonely, anxious existence. If you're feeling depleted, you have little to offer others. Your social circle can provide support. If not, find a new one. Holding on to what's gone or what didn't happen may put some in a victim mind-set. By releasing fear-based thoughts, you can soar to new heights. Without endings, you can't have new beginnings.

Princess of Cups

HIGH VIBE · Innocence, kindness, intuition, psychic energy, burgeoning sexuality

LOW VIBE · Immaturity, emotional instability, abandonment issues, depression

This Princess is an intuitive, empathetic, and youthful individual who may come bearing news. Often they're a friend who checks in at just the moment you need them. Thoughtful and imaginative, this archetype is often innately attuned to the needs and desires of others.

In relationship dynamics, the first blushes of infatuation with a person, place, or thing may be blooming. Some are discovering how they express love and what path leads to inner happiness. If you've met someone new, they're probably feeling equally smitten. You may be fielding offers of love, and singles will find that this is the perfect time to set some love intentions. Love is available to the open-hearted.

In professional life, you may be starting a training program or have recently landed an interview or job in a field you've long dreamed of. If not, new opportunities will present themselves in the near future. Keep on the lookout for possible mentors who can nurture your talent and keep your dreamy nature in check.

IF PULLED IN LOW VIBE · It's time to open up after emotionally sad or heavy times. Insecurity around intimacy and/or old wounds may be easily triggered at this time. Some may shut down, while others act out and fish for validation or communicate passive-aggressively. Confusion, depression, or self-involved behavior needs examination. Get your head out of the clouds, especially around romance and finances. It's time to extend your cup and welcome in new experiences.

Prince of Cups

HIGH VIBE · **Idealistic, emotional vulnerability, romantic, artistic vision, intuition, honesty, loyalty**

LOW VIBE · **Immaturity, neediness, emotional disconnection, manipulative, dysfunctional, narcissistic, depression**

This Prince is a charming, open-hearted, sensitive soul who leads with their emotions. This archetype can be an idealistic dreamer or a creative individual currently bringing a project or new idea into reality. If there's a decision to be made, let your intuitive side guide you. Keep an eye out for signs and messages along the way.

In relationship dynamics, this Prince makes a romantic, loving, loyal, emotionally available mate who is attentive to your needs. You may receive an offer of love or be contemplating offering up your cup. Some may feel a deepening connection to their current partner, while others are opening their hearts to love after an emotional shutdown and healing.

In professional life, new opportunities may be resparking your passion, clearing away past boredom. Some may have received a big clue to what path will lead to career advancement and emotional fulfillment. "Follow your bliss," as Joseph Campbell says, and remember to stay grounded while exploring new avenues for financial stability.

IF PULLED IN LOW VIBE · Moodiness, anxiety, and depression can leave the low-vibe Prince of Cups in a tailspin, or indicate an immature "mama's boy." Needy, clingy, or defensive and/or aloof behavior needs examination. Focus on what you want, not what is gone. If recent heartbreak, disappointments, or setbacks have steamrolled your joy, get back on the horse and out into the world again. There's a new path to travel, full of opportunity.

Queen of Cups

HIGH VIBE · Psychic energy, motherhood, sexuality, intuition, nature, emotional openness, nurturing

LOW VIBE · Emotional/sexual dysfunction, depression, self-indulgence, neediness

This Queen is an intuitive, receptive, loving, and nurturing soul with an open heart for honest, intimate spirit connection. They may be an empath or even slightly psychic; keep in touch with your logical side, lest you be ruled solely by your emotions. Empaths can be easily overwhelmed.

If representing a maternal figure in your life, this Queen's compassionate, emotionally available presence lifts you up when you need strength, but gives you space to grow into your own independent person. Generous with hugs, praise, and love, this Queen is an ideal nurturer.

In relationship dynamics, a connection on a deep soul level is available. Some might begin dating again after a break, while others recommit to a current partner. The Queen of Cups is a symbol of love and fertility and can sometimes indicate a pregnancy. If single, a potential love interest may appear—get ready.

In professional life, you may have landed the perfect interview or job, or be receiving recognition in your current position. You're feeling appreciated, supported, and valued. This may represent a boss or mentor who provides valuable support and encouragement. Seek their counsel and heed their advice. As a leader, this Queen may make some decisions based on sentiment. Stay on their good side by working up to potential.

IF PULLED IN LOW VIBE · Depression and anxiety can overwhelm, causing chaos. When triggered, stored emotional pain leads to self-doubt, lack of confidence, delusions, and a need for outside validation. This is the overbearing mother figure or clingy friend who drowns you in their pain. Remember, others feel their pain as deeply as you feel yours. Check in with your friends. Get back in touch with your intuition and what really makes you happy.

King of Cups

HIGH VIBE · **Romance, maturity, love, calm, focus, intuition, support, commitment**

LOW VIBE · **Depression, aloofness, neediness, aggression, imbalance, cruelty, apathy**

This King is a romantic, emotionally stable, supportive person, willing to lend an ear or shoulder to cry on when needed. This is the romantic leading man, the good guy who checks in on their feelings and yours. They might be a patron of the arts or a healer in touch with their feminine energy. They can be a great mate or friend, able to make you feel seen, supported, and appreciated.

If representing a paternal figure in your life, the sensitivity and support this King possesses provide connection and a profound understanding of the family's needs and dreams. Artistic expression and individuality are encouraged and celebrated. This is the kind of parent you can wrap around your finger, so be careful not to take advantage of their generous nature.

In relationship dynamics, this attractive romantic soul isn't in the dating pool long. When in love, they give their heart fully. Intuitively anticipating your desires, they understand the need for balance between career and love. They can come off a little too nice or accommodating, but try not to overlook them.

In professional life, you may be a compassionate leader or have just landed a dream meeting, gig, or bonus, and be feeling the love. In positions of power, this archetype takes into account the personal needs of others while still considering the bottom line. There may be someone around you who can provide mentorship. You'd be wise to take their advice.

IF PULLED IN LOW VIBE · Recent disappointments or intimacy issues may cause sadness, depression, anxiety, and/or feelings of neediness. For some, self-absorption, narcissism, and/or a lack of empathy may be hurting loved ones. You can't expect others to cater to your shifting moods. Stay emotionally balanced, and what you desire will find you.

Ace of Swords

HIGH VIBE · **Clarity, decisions, communication, confidence, assertiveness, breakthroughs**

LOW VIBE · **Confusion, insecurity, passivity, blocked energy, narrowness, negativity, conflict, obsessive thoughts**

Aces carry the potential of their whole suit, and in the case of Swords, that means that mental agility and brilliant ideas can strike at any time. This card represents the genesis of creative and analytical thinking, the kind that will move you closer to your goals. If a choice is on the table, this Ace can represent a resounding yes or a definitive no. Be confident your intuition will guide and align you with your higher purpose. Sudden epiphanies may strike.

In relationship dynamics, a clever individual who sparks your mental and physical interest may have entered the scene. For some, this is a moment of deeper commitment; for others, it's a sign to cut through the bullshit and get real. Communicate truthfully and prune away what isn't growing.

In professional life, clear and concise stewardship is needed to get the job done. A willingness to hear what others have to say makes you a natural leader. If unsure how to advance, refine your presentation skills and advocate for your ideas, and you're sure to shine. Newly imagined concepts may be just the ticket to success.

IF PULLED IN LOW VIBE · You might feel like you've hit a wall and find yourself confused, anxiety-ridden, defensive, overly emotional, and/or distant. If you feel like you're being gaslit, listen to what your intuition is telling you. This is the moment to clear a path for future successes and create your ideal life.

2 of Swords

HIGH VIBE · Decisions, clarity, stillness, reflection, balance, calm, serenity, deliberate inaction, boundaries

LOW VIBE · Indecision, confusion, stagnation, turning a blind eye, aloofness, an uneasy truce, stalemate

Stillness speaks. Take a time-out before making any big decisions. Get centered, and calm the anxious thoughts racing around your brain. You may need to set new boundaries with others. This is a time for passive restraint, as forcing issues in an aggressive manner won't give you the desired result.

In relationship dynamics, you may feel emotional disconnection or have attracted an aloof mate. Communication regarding intimacy styles and respect for the needs of others is key. Some may be dipping back into the dating pool after a period of healing and self-reflection. Others make the most of their personal time-out from love.

In professional life, a stalemate may be going on; contemplate all sides before making any final decrees. You may need to make decisions that require your full consideration before action. Learn when to voice opinions and when to hold your tongue. Some have been too passive and others too aggressive; find a middle ground.

IF PULLED IN LOW VIBE · Actively avoiding making decisions only creates more anxiety. Silence can send a powerful message, but willfully turning a blind eye may cause distress, anxiety, or passive-aggressive behavior. You may be feeling disconnected and isolated from the world outside. Intuit if current stasis is helping you gain perspective or keeping you stuck in the mud.

3 of Swords

HIGH VIBE · Release, closure, new love, moving on, renewal, recovery, healing

LOW VIBE · Disappointment, pain, heartbreak, loss, stagnation, limerence

Recent disappointments regarding work or your personal life may be bringing your vibe down. This is a heavy card, but at its best, it signals that your period of sadness or mourning is coming to a close, and valuable life lessons and new skills have been learned. The veil of brain fog is lifting; relief and reengagement with your heart are at hand. Release stagnant energy, thought patterns, and emotional entanglements that do not serve you. It's time to heal and open up your energy to new love and life experiences.

In relationship dynamics, old hurts are fading and your heart chakra is opening again after heartache. For some, current relationships are in crisis, and a frank, levelheaded discussion is needed to mend dynamics. If you're currently in separation or at an ending, try to lead with grace and compassion. Things may be ending, but cruelty or malice is low vibe. After healing, this might be a lifelong friend.

In professional life, a "no" can be the universe's way of protecting you. Hard knocks often give priceless insight and hone skills. Use these lessons to level up rather than act out. This is a reminder to remain positive despite difficulties.

IF PULLED IN LOW VIBE · Rejection and heartbreak may have caused a cycle of sadness, depression, anger, and anxiety. The result is stagnation, low self-esteem, and a feeling of hopelessness. Grieving and releasing is healthy, as long as you don't spin in that energy longer than needed. Address old patterns of behavior that kept you stuck and maybe even comfortable in low-vibe partnerships.

4 of Swords

HIGH VIBE · **Stability, mental time-out, self-care, peace, quiet, introspection**

LOW VIBE · **Aloof, distanced, rigid, anxiety, mental distress, chaos**

Sometimes it's best to say nothing and just digest what's going. A personal time-out and analytical repose allow space for reflection and expose what's working and what must be cut away. Consider what actions will build a solid foundation for the future. Some situations require a truce rather than a push for personal victory.

In relationship dynamics, some internal growth can only happen when processed alone. This is part of self-care; afterward, you and your partner will return replenished and reenergized. A redefining of boundaries may be happening. Some will discover that solitude works for them and choose to end a relationship. Others may hear from a former lover or friend who ghosted, or have a current interest disappear.

In professional life, you may need to pause, or take mini breaks throughout the day to keep your cool. Some are bored with the status quo or of working on their own. For others, a hitch in operations may necessitate a regrouping. If you've felt left out, power dynamics may be shifting for the better. Keep distractions to a minimum for optimum results.

IF PULLED IN LOW VIBE · You might feel disengaged from life or be partying too much and feel zoned out. Fear of failure or fear of success may have shut you down before you even got the chance to try. Self-protection, when taken too far, stems from insecurity, and plays out as aloofness, anger, or acting out in a passive-aggressive manner. It's time to heal. Don't be afraid to show the world who you've become and what you have to offer.

5 of Swords

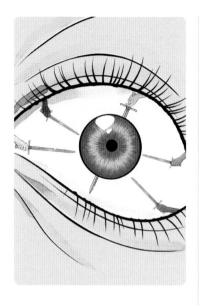

HIGH VIBE · Release, peace, ambition, hard-fought victory, forgiveness, truce, change

LOW VIBE · Struggle, bitterness, pettiness, aggression, cruelty, fighting, defensiveness

During times of struggle and strife, what do you gain if you keep on swinging? There's a choice at hand: defend your position or disengage completely. It's possible to defend without attacking and damaging others. Discern who and what needs your defense, and what should be cut away.

In relationship dynamics, you may have come to a place of peace after a period of discord. If you're not there yet, things will improve if you practice your listening skills and refrain from bulldozing your partner. Others, involved in bitter and repetitive arguments, feel a lack of connection. Cut through the nonsense and get back on the same team. For some, it might make more sense to walk away from a union stuck in combat mode.

In professional life, you may have pulled off a victory after a difficult battle, or are dealing with power struggles and dissent. Finding conflict-free solutions will score points and impress higher-ups. For others, your ambition is showing, and not necessarily in a good way. Stay out of office gossip and give your colleagues a chance to voice their ideas.

IF PULLED IN LOW VIBE · A sharp tongue and impenetrable defensive stance may be alienating you from people you care about. Paranoia, isolation, bursts of anger, and a need to be right at any cost carry low-vibe energy. Examine negative thought patterns and reactive behavior, and keep your ego in check. If you're always in the center of conflict and chaos, examine your part in those dynamics.

6 of Swords

HIGH VIBE · **Release, progress, healing, moving on, letting go, fortitude, transition**

LOW VIBE · **Pain, anxiety, defeat, failure, depression, chaos, refusal to let go**

When you choose to move away from situations that have caused you turmoil and pain, you inevitably end up closer to future joy. You may find yourself in a better headspace, able to see a new path after difficulties. The focus is on healing and releasing stagnant emotions rather than suppressing them. This enables a stronger connection to intuition, your higher self, and new opportunities.

In relationship dynamics, animosity may have subsided after a reconnection. You may appreciate new admirable qualities in your partner and reach a deeper level of understanding and love. For others, a final decision is made to either part ways or stay in a union. Surviving the lows can create a stronger, more integrated couple, capable of reaching higher highs.

In professional life, things may be back on track after a rough patch. Some may have recently landed jobs after an arduous search. Others are upping their game after lackluster reviews and rededicating energy to their craft.

IF PULLED IN LOW VIBE · Anxiety, depression, anger, and mental confusion can take over when you've been staring into the abyss of past sorrows for too long. If you continue to spin in what was or wasn't, you'll find it impossible to move forward into a new reality. Don't be afraid to ask for help from friends when you need it. This transition period is guiding you to a more fulfilling life. It's time to move to your happy place.

7 of Swords

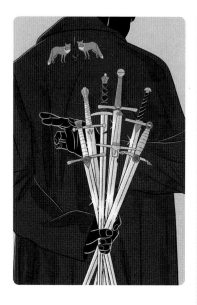

HIGH VIBE · Cunning, stealth, analysis, clarity, purpose, shrewdness, cleverness

LOW VIBE · Selfishness, theft, manipulation, trickery, false friends, secrets, deception

Whatever the situation at hand, keep plans and pertinent information to yourself while you suss out the motivations of others as well as your own. Don't tip your hand to those who'd bite it. Advance, stay in integrity, and keep your wits about you. You'll get the desired results quicker.

In relationship dynamics, a communication checkup may be in order. Are you or your partner unable to forgive a betrayal or currently being manipulative? Game playing, half-truths, and secrets may come to light and help clear the air or break a few hearts. If you've recently met someone new, get all the details; you may not have the full picture.

In professional life, sometimes the prudent thing to do is hold back and formulate a better plan, despite the urge to rush in. There may be a delicate situation rife with backstabbing and competition creating dissension. Stay high vibe, and don't resort to malice or trickery despite tempting shortcuts. Analyze how to massage rather than manipulate a win, and keep your eyes open for a fox in the henhouse.

IF PULLED IN LOW VIBE · You may be on the receiving or giving end of a betrayal after a period of gaslighting. For others, sneaky efforts to jump ahead of the pack may have compromised morals. It's time to adjust. Trickery and deceit on the way up the ladder of career, relationship, or spiritual advancement only get you so far before low-vibe truths are revealed. Have faith that your smarts and mental fortitude will see you through to better days.

8 of Swords

HIGH VIBE · **Choice, confidence, sure-footedness, determination, acceptance, movement**

LOW VIBE · **Indecision, feeling stuck, no options, anxiety, insecurity, passivity**

You may be realizing it's possible to extricate yourself from a thorny situation and clear a path for new growth. Confidence is returning after a period of doubt or feelings of victimization. Surrendering to what is, and leaving behind what's been lost, clears away atrophy. The power to change your circumstances is within you.

In relationship dynamics, emotional breakthroughs help move you into a more loving and connected vibe. Heaviness may be lifting, allowing joy and a sense of play to sneak back in. Others may be attached to toxic situations that no longer bring pleasure. Quiet your mind chatter and spinning anxiety, take off the blinders, and make a choice to put happiness first.

In professional life, dwelling on what previously went wrong is slowing your roll. Or you may have just found the solution to a thorny problem, allowing movement after stasis. Regroup and attack the problem from a different angle. Some may be realizing they're unfulfilled in a dead-end situation and make plans to switch career paths.

IF PULLED IN LOW VIBE · The bonds tying you to a difficult person, place, or thing are self-imposed. Refusing to take responsibility for your part in where you've ended up is keeping you stuck. Stop blaming others for your station in life and focus on what is in your power to change. Some prisons are of our own making; acknowledge this truth, and free yourself.

9 of Swords

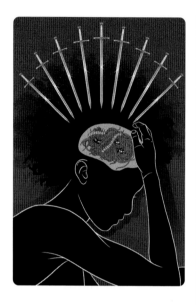

In relationship dynamics, this card can signify insecurity in a dating situation. Is this an old anxiety pattern, or do current circumstances validate your fear? Others may finally feel safe to drop the mask and reveal intimate details. When you let others in on who you really are and what you truly desire, you'll attract someone who can appreciate your many juxtapositions.

In professional life, the going may be tricky. Remaining centered is the goal. Logic and analytical thought will help you rise above the fray. Fear of failure or success can wreak havoc on your self-esteem; reach out to mentors and colleagues for help through any rough patches.

HIGH VIBE · **Release, peace, clarity, resolution, decisiveness, spirit connection**

LOW VIBE · **Anxiety, depression, loss of hope, lack of faith, dark night of the soul**

This is colloquially known as the anxiety card. The good thing is, the worst of what's happening currently is the spinning anxiety plaguing your mind. This doesn't mean your problems aren't real, but rather that your current coping methods are no longer working. Much of what's plaguing you is fear-based thinking.

IF PULLED IN LOW VIBE · If you're in a spin-out, it may be indicative of inaction or the constant replay of past foibles. When fear, self-loathing, and depression become debilitating, decipher what's real and what's coming from your inner low vibe. Old trauma can feel overpowering and cause a shutdown. If incessant negative thought patterns are dragging you down, reach out for help. Talk therapy is a great way to process feelings. You have the power to shift your reality with your thoughts; take it and run to greener pastures.

10 of Swords

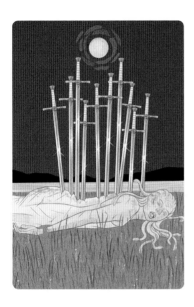

HIGH VIBE · Completion, closure, endings, release, conclusion, new beginnings

LOW VIBE · Loss, endings, separation, divorce, breakups, rejection, disappointment

Even in high vibe, this is one of the tarot's heavy cards; real-world loss was experienced. Yet, for most, the worst has already happened. Acceptance of what is rather than what's been lost brings forward movement. A "dark night of the soul" can herald professional, personal, and spiritual rebirth. Some experiences are finite; letting go gracefully makes way for fertile new opportunities.

In relationship dynamics, a past connection thought long gone may appear with an offer of renewed interest, while for others, a difficult patch has ended. The natural lifespan of people in our orbit can be finite at best. Celebrate and appreciate what you have while you have it. In its lower vibe, this card can mean a stale relationship has been over for a while, and holding on is causing emotional pain. You can attract a significant other who matches your vibe once the specter of the past is no longer haunting you.

In professional life, a contract or job may have closed out; stay alert for new opportunities. For those experiencing difficulties, remember you're building a more secure foundation for the future, and it's imperative not to obsess over what could have been. Keep your eyes on the prize and your energy moving forward.

IF PULLED IN LOW VIBE · A loss of spiritual faith, a financial dilemma, or the dissolution of a relationship can cause deep soul hurt. Refusing to accept reality feeds depression and anxiety. Endings are never easy, but they are a natural part of our lives. If you're alone, isolated, and feeling abandoned or hopeless, it's time to check in with your circle, a therapist, or a trusted mentor. Cut out what's no longer working and make space for new experiences and mutual love.

Princess of Swords

HIGH VIBE · Confidence, analytical mind, curiosity, wit, opinionated, intelligence

LOW VIBE · Aloof, petty, vindictive, mind games, self-centeredness, thoughtlessness, anxiety

This Princess is a whip-smart force of nature, brimming with ideas and no shortage of words to convey them. Carrying a burgeoning awareness of their innate powers, they are ready for action. A mercurial nature means ideologies may change without warning. They can lose interest and appear distant when bored. Princess cards can often be message bearers, and this Princess brings unexpected news, and for some, a change of plans.

In relationship dynamics, this is a witty, entertaining partner, who values a keen mind, decisive action, and spirited debate. When caught up in their head or preoccupied with self, they can appear aloof and moody. For some, speaking without thought can be an issue. If you learn to communicate your needs, this can be an intelligent companion to grow and learn with.

In professional life, this bright, opinionated idea maker is an asset to any team. They can be a bit of a know-it-all and would benefit from listening rather than speaking. Immaturity may cause them to cut and run, rather than problem-solve. Mentorship can help nourish their analytical mind and let them flourish.

**IF PULLED IN LOW VIBE · **Inside, this Princess is dying for connection to something or someone greater than themselves. Speaking with a sharp tongue, gossiping, or cutting others down can be a cover for insecurity. Feelings of superiority and lack of empathy can create a state of anxiety. Hyping yourself up to others can be good, but showing them what you can do through your actions is better.

Prince of Swords

HIGH VIBE · Intelligence, ideas, visionary, analytical thinking, wittiness, rapid expansion

LOW VIBE · Egocentric, lack of clarity, unmotivated, unpredictability, reckless behavior, lack of foresight, impulsivity

This Prince is a spirited and full-of-action person who enjoys a healthy debate or exchange of ideas. When this archetype uses their innovative powers for good, they can change the world. Swords are the most analytical suit, but here, there's a tendency to charge in without thinking issues through. They can be more focused on the outcome than on the process, which can be a handicap in the long run. Critical analysis and targeted action are at your disposal; focus your ambition and drive on specific goals.

In relationship dynamics, an intellectually stimulating partner may be keeping you preoccupied. Diligent in pursuing what they desire, this archetype may become aloof, self-focused, and judgmental of others when overwhelmed or underappreciated. Mercurial in nature, they can disappear when bored. If you're lucky enough to capture their mind, their heart will follow.

In professional life, your mental acumen is on point; solutions may come easily at this time. Fact-find before processing any major decisions. Even if your mind's set, a forward-thinking individual with novel concepts may provide the breakthrough you need.

**IF PULLED IN LOW VIBE · A tendency to be brash, controlling, argumentative, or narrow-minded may have you cutting out situations that could help advance your station. For some, mental confusion or a lack of drive may cause emotional disconnect or a defensiveness that alienates. Being overly critical of others is a reflection of your own harsh inner dialogue. Let go of being angry about what didn't go your way. Clear away negative thought patterns and focus on what you can accomplish.

Queen of Swords

HIGH VIBE · **Clarity, ideas, fairness, maturity, fortitude, insight**

LOW VIBE · **Anxiety, depression, confusion, narrowness, cruelty, judgment**

This Queen leads with a levelheaded intelligence and values directness in communication. Seldom swayed by emotions, their logical insights and practical guidance make them invaluable in any situation. Quick-witted and clever, they won't back down from an argument. They may inadvertently bruise egos and feelings with their blunt approach—don't take it personally.

If this Queen represents a maternal figure in your life, this archetype is fiercely protective and deeply caring, often keenly keyed in to the differing needs of their loved ones. Not always the most outwardly affectionate, emotional manipulation or sentimentality will tend to lower their opinion of you.

In relationship dynamics, they are a strong-willed, independent person, comfortable expressing their opinions and desires and setting boundaries. Remember to open your heart, as well as your mouth, when dealing with them. If bored or unfulfilled, they may cut off contact without much notice.

In professional life, this Queen is in their element: a confident, detail-oriented leader, capable of making decisions that benefit all concerned. Intuition and clear communication leave little room for misunderstandings or being taken advantage of. Though it may not be in your nature, let others express their viewpoints so you can get all the facts before making judgment calls. Speak up, but not at the expense of others.

IF PULLED IN LOW VIBE · There may be a lack of clarity in your life. Cruel and cutting verbal jabs can be a defense mechanism that isolates you, and indicate issues of control and low self-esteem. If you're in a pattern of communicating through bickering and arguing, work on shifting this. Replaying a loop of negative thoughts isn't helping. Use your considerable powers for good; open up your mind to open up your world.

King of Swords

This King has wisdom to impart and words to motivate. With a turn of phrase, they can convert others to their way of thinking; this is a gift that puts them in the seat of power. Rarely swayed by sentiment, they'll provide wise counsel, but won't suffer fools lightly. If this card represents you, communicate your ideas clearly to achieve your goals.

If it represents a paternal figure in your life, this King fiercely protects their loved ones. Their innate code of ethics demands high standards, which they expect you to live up to. Though not as demonstrative as some of the other Kings, they are willing to show affection and love to those they value, and have the acumen to decipher the unique needs of those they love.

In relationship dynamics, this fascinating individual can provide hours of conversation and a strong mental and physical connection. They make a loyal partner. Be sure to connect your head and heart energy if the relationship is at a sticking point. Speak honestly, as subterfuge will only complicate dynamics.

In professional life, do your research before wasting this King's time. Asking them something you could have found out on your own will only lower their opinion of you. Showing initiative will make them more likely to extend help in the future. If you're in charge, give others a voice and they'll champion you.

IF PULLED IN LOW VIBE · A short temper, control issues, and anxiety may cause emotional distance and a narrow view of the world. Lack of clarity or an apathetic nature will keep you disconnected from others. It's time to open up and see things through a different prism.

Ace of Discs

may land you in a great situation. If no gains have presented themselves yet, stay on task, and trust that seeds planted will soon mature. You're due for a break, specifically a financial one.

In relationship dynamics, you may have met a new partner whose lifestyle meshes with your own. Discs are the most practical suit, so you may be dealing with logistics, like moving in or making a big purchase together. Practical people can be overlooked, especially when there's flashier "Wand" energy out there. If you're longing for monogamy and stability, practical people make great mates. Some may welcome a new addition to the family. If single, you're sure to shine and attract new potential partners.

In professional life, a leg up is on the way. Pay attention, as new avenues of revenue are coming; don't let them pass you by. Wealth can be attracted, so don't slack off. Prioritize where energy and resources are invested. The universe wants to reward your ambition and hard work.

HIGH VIBE · Success, abundance, security, new beginnings, wealth, inheritance, independence, opportunity

LOW VIBE · Failure, anxiety, materialism, instability, shallowness, financial duress, blocked energy

Aces carry the potential of their whole suit, and in the case of Discs, this means a fertile time ripe with financial and personal potential. There's more to come if you stay grounded and pay attention to incoming messages and opportunities. Unexpected news

IF PULLED IN LOW VIBE · Financial instability is devastating when there's no backup plan. If you're counting on a big payday or spending without thought, this is your reminder to do a financial reality check before things go pear-shaped. Invest in yourself, and no one can stop you.

2 of Discs

HIGH VIBE · **Balance, finances, effort, hard work, decisions, practical matters, multitasking**

LOW VIBE · **Lack of control, poverty, imbalance, greed, laziness, fiscal struggle**

There may be a lot thrown at you during this time, but the good news is that you have the discipline, ambition, and stamina to juggle more than a few projects. Your acumen and skills are being tested, but know that you're up to the task. Make the most of opportunities and seek balance in work and personal life. Life is a constant cycle of give and take. Resisting this is futile. Learning to ride the ups and downs with grace is the lesson this card suggests.

In relationship dynamics, a comfortable, balanced groove with your partner or someone new means you're invested emotionally. Money issues may arise; honest communication about what's realistic and what's not will keep boundaries clear. Some may be juggling more than one partner.

In professional life, there's a need to cut out distractions and focus on the projects at hand. Leveling up means having to take on more responsibilities. How you handle them now determines how quickly you'll advance in your chosen field. Some opportunities may come and go. Keep your eyes forward. Learning how to prioritize will be fundamental.

IF PULLED IN LOW VIBE · Get honest about emotional and financial behaviors that are draining you. And get real about your extraneous spending if you find yourself running short on funds every month. The daily grind has some overwhelmed. Others are distracting themselves rather than focusing on their career path, slowing financial gain. Everybody feels unsure and unsteady when starting a new profession. Remember to seek balance as you take on more, and you'll soar.

3 of Discs

HIGH VIBE · **Craftsmanship, teamwork, hard work, planning stages, mentorship, collaboration**

LOW VIBE · **Laziness, incompatibility, ego, conflict, disorganization, lack of motivation**

Aspirations are in the planning stages; recently gained skills are useful, as are partnerships formed with people you can learn from and grow with. You may have a new circle of friends or new business partnerships that elevate your game. If you're still struggling, opportunities will present themselves, landing you in a position to see your vision to fruition. Break out of the daily grind and invest time in new activities. This card is a reminder that you are not an island, and you'll often reach greater heights with the help of others.

In relationship dynamics, you may be meeting a slew of suitors. Bear in mind that the person who holds your interest may have similar options. Some partnerships have hit their stride. For others, things may be shifting. If you're feeling left out, exercising patience and compassion will go a long way. Be open to new ways of connecting.

In professional life, your hard work and ego sacrifices have not gone unnoticed. Progress and some recognition may net you a mentor or the eye of an investor who sees your vision. Group dynamics can often be competitive, and learning to voice ideas in a way that makes others willing to listen will serve you. Outside opinions can help refine talent. For those dealing with difficult coworkers, do not let them push your buttons or throw your focus off the endgame.

IF PULLED IN LOW VIBE · You may feel underappreciated and overlooked despite the tremendous amount of effort you've exerted. This is not the time to lose motivation or isolate yourself. Seek out sage advice and stay on task: victory is coming. Let go of outdated methodology and invest in working with others to refine your dreams.

4 of Discs

HIGH VIBE · **Stability, solitude, protection, self-preservation, peace, introspection**

LOW VIBE · **Instability, isolation, selfishness, pride, defensive, instability, narrowness**

Reconnection through introspection is front and center. Taking a pause to reassess is self-care, and this is the time to do it. Set boundaries if you need to. Invest time on a single goal; rein in and focus, even when others try to distract you. Think about investments wisely; err on the side of frugality and you should make it through any tough spots.

In relationship dynamics, things may feel secure, stable, and even routine. Some may need to give their partner space; don't take it personally. If you're bothered by their validly busy schedule, find a hobby, or examine codependent patterns. With that said, there's a difference between having boundaries and emotional withholding. Make sure you're clear on what's what.

In professional life, you may need to hole up and diligently work on a project. Missing out on a few social events will pay off in the long run. You may be feeling secure and comfortable at work, understanding the value you bring to the team and your place on it. Be sure to share the spotlight with coworkers. To avoid burnout, take a personal day, if needed.

IF PULLED IN LOW VIBE · Stinginess, defensiveness, and control issues can derail plans if you're not careful. Take others into consideration, expand your horizons, and focus on manifesting the kind of life you've always envisioned. Those who've withdrawn can awaken to how isolated they've become, surrounded by possessions that can't give or receive love. Open up your world.

5 of Discs

HIGH VIBE · Financial stability, charity, savings, tolerance, kindness, status, spirituality

LOW VIBE · Bad luck, loss, greed, financial ruin, cruelty, crisis, scarcity, selfishness

Fortune, status, and security are always in flux, and the prudent prepare for either side of the coin. Recent upheavals may have your back up against a wall. Tighten your belt and focus on what's in your power to shift. Develop a workable plan of action, rather than flights of fancy or indulgence in feelings of failure. Some may have realized that financial success alone does not guarantee happiness. Compassion for yourself and an awareness of the plight of others may help give perspective.

In relationship dynamics, this card, at its best, can signify a reconnection after a period of being out in the cold. Love is there, but it needs nurturing to flourish. Others may be setting down anger and bitterness for love. For some couples, financial instability may cause tension and anxiety, affecting dynamics. Remember the reasons you fell in love, and you should be able to get back on solid ground.

In professional life, new income streams can come in after a period of instability. Don't celebrate just yet; continue to check where you allocate money to stay in the black. Be diligent on the hunt for additional revenue streams. Others may need to put pride and ego aside to find and ask for help. Ground yourself and lift the vibration by volunteering time to a cause you support. You'll gain perspective.

IF PULLED IN LOW VIBE · Anxiety, depression, fear, and conflict around past or present emotional and financial mistakes can hold you back. For others, stinginess, lack of compassion, and miserly behavior can isolate. Gratification and reconnection to your higher self comes when in service to the collective as a whole. New opportunities for growth will present themselves to those who remain optimistic.

6 of Discs

HIGH VIBE · **Opportunity, relief, abundance, charity, generosity**

LOW VIBE · **Scarcity, selfishness, low ambition, fear of failure or success**

New offers in all areas may be coming in and going out. This is when all the hard work begins to pay off. What's started now may lead to a huge payoff. Opportunities abound when you remain open to outside help. If there's a bird in hand, grab it—if the terms are right. If nothing's shifted yet, there's a chance you're overlooking an opening right in front of your face.

In relationship dynamics, you may have a new interest offering friendship or love. Others find more harmonious ways to communicate, live, and work together. Some may experience a rejection or feel a partner has all the power; know your value and stay aware of the many other viable possibilities around.

In professional life, you may be mid-negotiation on a deal; stay the course. This is an opportune time for new partnerships. A boss or outside investor may back your ideas. Stay focused and grounded; don't let pride or ego hold you back from accepting help. Power imbalances can challenge the ego, so keep yours in check for a positive change of fate.

IF PULLED IN LOW VIBE · Rethink ideas that aren't working, and examine belief patterns that may be suppressing your personal power. Replaying perceived failures lowers your vibe. Ask rather than demand help of others, and actively participate in your own recovery and success. We are only as strong as our weakest fellow man. Invest in yourself, and others will follow.

7 of Discs

HIGH VIBE · Progress, development, planning, waiting period, beginning of manifestation, hard work, assessment, dedication

LOW VIBE · Impatience, narrowness, lack of ambition, poor planning, failure, frustration

You may be gestating something that requires constant nurturing and your full attention. Stay the course! Continue on with patience, perseverance, and attention to detail. You've come far—put your hustle on what needs fine-tuning. Trust that you're on the right track; keep focused on long-term goals and you'll see a solid payoff.

In relationship dynamics, let things flourish naturally. Balance can be found, if desired; find appreciation in where you're at. Nourish what's present, and don't push too hard for enormous leaps forward just yet. Control issues, powers struggles, and anxiety about the future may arise.

In professional life, seeds previously planted are beginning to show returns, though the pace may be far too languid for some, causing frustration. You may feel like you're in the doldrums, but you're progressing more than you think. Don't spend money you haven't earned yet; this is a crucial time to double down and check details to ensure a bountiful harvest. If things feel on uneven footing, a cooler head will prevail.

IF PULLED IN LOW VIBE · Lack of recognition or acknowledgment can cause discontent, aggravation, restlessness, and ingratitude. Past disappointments and sadness may overwhelm. Ask if a defeating attitude and fearful thought patterns are dragging you down, or if you're investing energy into dead ends. What you put out is what you attract in. Gratitude will create the best environment for new growth.

8 of Discs

HIGH VIBE · **Drive, labor, recognition, progress, craftsmanship, quality, advancement**

LOW VIBE · **Lack of drive, laziness, boredom, disconnect, depression**

Your ambition and hard work are about to pay off big. Some may even have found a new spiritual connection to their craft. Higher-ups or those in a position to help you are noting your ambition and drive. Rewards are coming now and further down the line. Trust that the universe sees how valuable your contributions are.

In relationship dynamics, the investments you've put into your emotional connections are showing. Some couples understand what it takes for a successful union and are working well together. Others may be moving out of the infatuation stage and into a more substantial connection with a partner. This is the time to figure out if a potential mate is worth the energy, or is just a surface infatuation.

In professional life, put in your 10,000 hours to up your expertise and become a master of your craft. You may be apprenticing or working for a demanding boss—show them you're dedicated and up to the challenge. Don't worry about workplace gossip; keep your nose to the grindstone and let your work speak for itself. While success is never fully guaranteed, diligence and focus are rewarded.

IF PULLED IN LOW VIBE · You may feel underappreciated, undervalued, and overworked. Stay realistic about finances and have faith that relief and rewards are coming. Check in on where you're investing your energy, as distractions may be slowing momentum. Be realistic about which situations lead to dead ends and which raise your vibe and connect you to spirit. Develop your skill sets and show the world your talents.

9 of Discs

HIGH VIBE · **Investments, prosperity, solitude, replenishment, materialism, self-reliance, leisure, comfort, security**

LOW VIBE · **Greed, loneliness, isolation, instability, insecurity, lack of money, boredom, discomfort**

The solid foundation you've laid has created a welcome new fabulous reality. Abundance abounds; if life has been all work and no play, indulge and pamper yourself—you've earned it. Some may find they've been hyper focused on business and there's no one around to celebrate with. Invest your time into things and people that bring you joy.

In relationship dynamics, you may be enjoying a comfortable home life, abundant with love. With that said, this is often referred to as "the single person's card." They enjoy their own company and aren't necessarily looking for a partner. After a time-out, some unattached people may want to jump back into the dating pool. Manifesting your heart's desire is possible at this time.

In professional life, lucrative opportunities are on the way or may have already arrived. Ideas have become tangible, money-making realities. Celebrate the fruits of your labor. Invest time and money wisely for big future returns. Attachments to possessions or taking all the credit for the team's efforts may cause isolation.

IF PULLED IN LOW VIBE · Feelings of isolation and loneliness may result from being overly self-protective and living a lifestyle of accumulation. Spending money rashly and living above your means can come back to haunt. Take action before feelings of depression, worthlessness, or self-aggrandizement set in. Jealousy and envy may arise when comparing yourself to others or vice versa. Stay in gratitude when hard work shows dividends, and share the wealth. Hubris will bring you down; gratitude lifts you up.

10 of Discs

HIGH VIBE · **Success, victory, joy, harmony, giving birth to something greater than yourself, accumulation**

LOW VIBE · **Loss, failure, discord, struggle, disappointment, release, sadness, defeat**

The culmination of your hard work has arrived; it's time to celebrate your many successes. A major personal victory or a business coup has propelled you into the future of your dreams. Things may be different than you imagined, but you're exactly where you're supposed to be. Celebrations of all manner are in order. Weddings, graduations, and other momentous occasions may be marked.

In relationship dynamics, there's a happily-ever-after joyful feeling; things are coming together just as you dreamed. Others may be moving in with a partner, or possibly out. Hopefully you're both on the same page as culminations unfurl. For most, this is a joyous time, when the living is easy.

In professional life, this is a card of financial success and gain. A major project may be reaching completion, with satisfaction on all fronts. If you're waiting on a lucrative payday, be sure to share the victory with those who championed your dreams. For others, anticipation is high as deals are finalized. Wait until the money is in your pocket before spending it.

IF PULLED IN LOW VIBE · If there's been an unwanted ending, trust that the situation was not ideal for you in the long run. When things don't pan out the way we expect, it's hard to see the bright side. It may be time to let go of a dream or a vision you see little to no progress on. Loss needs to be mourned and feelings of failure processed to make way for future success. And sometimes, even acquiring everything you thought you wanted can leave you feeling empty. New beginnings are on the way; take time to appreciate how far you've come.

Princess of Discs

HIGH VIBE · **Hard work, focus, financial acuity, practical matters**

LOW VIBE · **Lack of drive, low ambition, frivolity, financial loss**

This Princess is a solid, reliable person, with an eye on practical matters and our connection to the planet. They rarely get lost in distractions or illusions. Planning, foresight, hard work, and some frugality give them the power to manifest dreams into reality. This Princess focuses on developing their skill set and innate talents. Princesses in general are message bearers; news of a job opportunity or acceptance to a program that will benefit your goals may come your way.

In relationship dynamics, a dependable partner with a mind for practicality and details may present. Trust, loyalty, and commitment are important to this occasionally too-tied-up-in-work archetype. When their heart and mind are mentally and physically engaged, they provide stability and love for a strong, peaceful union.

In professional life, this hardworking individual will give their all and put in long hours on the task at hand. Mentorship with a seasoned associate would be advantageous. It's time to pursue every avenue available that furthers your goals while being realistic about your finances. This is the beginning of building a stable foundation.

IF PULLED IN LOW VIBE · Ego-based thinking can equate personal power with outward status and accumulation of assets. Insecurity, self-loathing, or impractical behavior can signal that you're out of touch. This is not a time for risks—there's no room for reckless spending. For some, there's a need to step back from an overload of responsibilities, while others need to look at a tendency to shirk duties. Get grounded and have faith that with proper effort, your goals are attainable.

Prince of Discs

HIGH VIBE · Hard work, determination, grounded, practicality, responsibility, frugality

LOW VIBE · Scattered energy, lack of drive, depression, flightiness, laziness

This Prince is a responsible, grounded, practical individual you can count on in a pinch. Innately they understand that helping others creates a higher vibration. This is the most plodding Prince in the deck, but slow and steady wins the race. Cumulative progress and a pragmatic outlook give solid results and a sense of accomplishment and freedom.

In relationship dynamics, this commitment-minded partner makes a fantastic provider and supportive mate. It's often said that this is the only Prince to cross the finish line, if you're marriage-minded. More straightforward than romantic, they can be easy to overlook. This is the archetypal salt-of-the-earth good soul who's attentive, staid, and reliable. Once you train them in your love and romance language, their loyalty and devotion will be priceless.

In professional life, work dynamics should be progressing nicely, if, for some, slowly. More responsibilities mean longer hours, but are a sign that the boss appreciates your diligent work ethic. Keep a practical eye on your savings, but don't forget to layer in a little fun, or life can become dull. This is a good time to open an investment account.

IF PULLED IN LOW VIBE · A feeling of discontent or boredom with the daily grind can blunt the senses. Shake up the status quo while keeping an eye on your responsibilities and your pocketbook. There may be feelings of resentment or a fear of failure or success causing things to stall out. Check in on how motivated you are. Stay on task, but not to the point of rigidity. In time, the investment in yourself will pay off big.

Queen of Discs

HIGH VIBE · **Generosity, practicality, fortune, opportunity, refinement, luxury**

LOW VIBE · **Greed, cruelty, ego, financial setback, bad business, materialism**

This Queen is a successful, down-to-earth person, fully aware of their value, accomplishments, and status. Financially savvy, they remain open-hearted, with a spirited sense of generosity. This archetype exceeds when helping others, rather than hoarding their gifts away.

If representing a maternal figure in your life, this Queen is Mother Earth: a nurturing, loving caregiver who encourages you to find your own path. They instinctively understand how a healthy sense of self furthers you in life. They cheer your wins, support your efforts, give you love, and voice opinions when necessary.

In relationship dynamics, this thoughtful, grounded, empathetic mate possesses an earthy sexuality. If you speak of love but your behavior doesn't back it up, they'll break things off, confident there's someone more present available. Some may stop playing around and decide to find their emotional and intellectual equal.

In professional life, you may see a promotion, and more responsibilities, at your current job. Some may be adapting to a new position at the head of the table. A shrewd boss or mentor may be keen to help you move up the ranks; if there's a question or decision to be made, bend their ear. If things are tight financially, turn a firm eye to where money is allocated and pinch some pennies.

IF PULLED IN LOW VIBE · The Queen of Discs is a reminder to be practical in matters of the heart and finances. Shortsightedness, selfishness, and acting out judgmentally toward others can only cause friction. What you nurture will provide you with shelter.

King of Discs

HIGH VIBE · **Power, generosity, practicality, fortune, abundance, prosperity**

LOW VIBE · **Greed, cruelty, loss, pompous nature, ego, setback**

This King is a successful, business-savvy individual who commands respect. Ambition, talent, and tangible gains have created emotional and financial stability. Maturity around who and what you invest time and finances in will pay off. Stay the course, plan ahead, and victory is yours!

If representing a paternal figure in your life, this protective King is the archetype of a provider and dedicated family person. Some may find their methods controlling, but should still actively seek their wise counsel on practical matters.

In relationship dynamics, this loyal partner can provide dependable love and support. Usually straightforward in communication, they expect the same from you and are sure to provide a stable environment to flourish in. If things feel routine, activities outside the norm can help you reconnect with your partner.

In professional life, the perfect backer for your dream scheme may have appeared. Take them up on their offer. For others, a tough, exacting boss may have singled you out for praise and new responsibilities. Keep up the effort, and rewards should start coming in. If you're due a windfall, set some of it aside and then celebrate.

IF PULLED IN LOW VIBE ·
Irresponsibility around finances may have you in a tough spot. Anxiety or feelings of failure may prevent forward movement. There may be an imbalance of power with a controlling parent or partner who holds the purse strings. Take an active role in owning your part in what's going on in your world. New opportunities are available—it's time to ground yourself, focus, and become who you're meant to be.